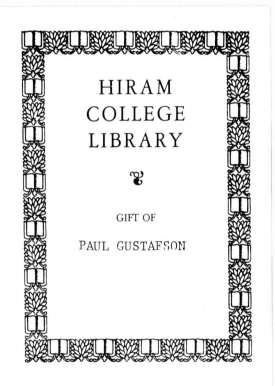

CHILDREN OF THE CUMBERLAND

CHILDREN

OF THE

CUMBERLAND

By CLAUDIA LEWIS

PHOTOGRAPHS BY
WILLIAM T. BUTTRICK, JR.

NEW YORK 1946

COLUMBIA UNIVERSITY PRESS

THIS BOOK IS PRESENTED AS PART OF THE PROGRAM OF THE
DIVISION OF STUDIES AND PUBLICATIONS
OF THE BANK STREET SCHOOLS, 69 BANK STREET, NEW YORK

TO THE MEMORY OF
WILLIAM T. BUTTRICK, Jr.

The names used throughout this study are commonly found in the regions concerned, but only those of Dr. Lillian Johnson, Miss May Justus, and Mr. Kilgore are the correct names of the people to whom they refer. Place names in the Tennessee locality are fictitious.

FOREWORD

THE NEW EDUCATION with which we have been experimenting since the turn of the century is maturing rapidly. Perhaps clearest evidence for this is the increased discussion of the problems still to be solved. Prominent among these are questions such as the clearer definition of freedom, how much release of hostile feeling has true therapeutic value, where is the borderline at which free expression of hostility through aggression, instead of being healthy as release, becomes anxiety-producing by generating deeper levels of guilt. How much does authoritative discipline injure the natural spontaneity and creativeness of the growing child? What will injure or strengthen a child's feeling of security and do we want security at any price?

These and many others were the problems in our minds when Miss Lewis, who had been one of our students in The Cooperative School for Teachers and one of our teachers in the Harriet Johnson Nursery School, came back from Summerville with her challenging observations of the children she had been teaching there and how different they were from the New York City children she had left behind. When it was decided that this material should be systematized and studied because of its vital implications for psychology and education, we had no idea that a book such as this one would be the outcome.

Apart from the light it throws on the particular questions that are raised, analyzed and discussed, the book has values that are important for the future of research and writing in this field. It demonstrates with a new clarity how essential it is that studies of children should be studies of *children-in-their-life-situations*. It describes and analyzes not so much the behavior of the children as their reactions to the influences impinging upon them, and in so much provides a healthy antidote to the errors and fallacies of the "norm" approach to the understanding of child development.

The experience of the war years has sharpened the need for this approach. Teachers who had taught middle-class city children for years found themselves surprised and often perplexed by the children who came to them in the child care centers, from other economic and cultural groups in the same cities. School systems are now working on the revision of curriculum in the direction of adapting it to the maturity levels and needs of children. They are facing the dilemma of how to plan for all the first graders, who come from a wide range of differing neighborhoods and family life backgrounds. The material on "Rosalie" included in this study represents a precursor of a problem which has in the last few years become foremost wherever educators are concerned with the fundamental process of growth and learning.

Perhaps one of the most distinctive contributions of a book such as this one lies in the technique of presentation. Though serious and weighty questions are posed from the start, the chapters unfold a story about living people and their children, written with all the delicacy and sensitive penetration that true life stories deserve. The reader, consequently, has the rich and satisfying experience of knowing the material firsthand and the unusual opportunity to think along with the author. So many books give us only the overdigested end-products, and make of reading a much less creative process than it needs to be. Conceivably, not all the readers of this book will agree with the conclusions which Miss Lewis draws from the analysis of her observations. The value lies in the fact that the material is so fully and graphically presented that there is room for readers to think about it, agree or disagree, or check these findings with similar experience of their own.

In studies of this kind, the personality of the research worker is an important factor. I have heard Miss Lewis regret some of the gaps in her material and express the wish that this or that

idea could have been more fully documented. And it may well
be that someone else might have returned with data on areas
which Miss Lewis was not willing to probe. What she presents
represents the limits that were natural and acceptable to her and
which she was not willing to transgress while she lived among
the Summerville people and taught their little children. It represents her way of adapting to their code. This is a problem in
technique which will be of growing importance not only for
studies of groups but for studies of individuals as well. It is tied
up with the current search for ways of studying and analyzing
behavior that will reveal the mainsprings and the origins as well
as the surface manifestations. Perhaps we are approaching the
time when the description of the situation in which a study is
being made will have to include not only the people studied and
the nature of their situations but also some data on the nature
of the person making the study.

The problems discussed in the book have widespread relevance.
They are of concern to the parent who wonders whether the
conflicts which his child faces are essentially different from those
which shadowed his own childhood, to the teacher who ponders
over how most successfully to bring out the creative potential of
her group, to the psychologist who is at work on the problems
of socialization of the individual, to the sociologist who is analyzing the relation between social mores and family life. That they
are presented through these moving descriptions of human beings can only be considered a matter of unusual good fortune.

BARBARA BIBER

New York
July, 1946

PREFACE

✿✿✿✿✿✿✿✿✿✿✿✿✿✿✿✿✿✿✿✿✿✿✿✿✿

IF ONE STOPPED TO THINK of it in that way, one could picture a map of the United States in terms of its children—not necessarily a flat map on a page with black dots for the Negro children in the South, yellow for the Orientals in California, and brown for the Indians of the Southwest. Rather, I am thinking of that imaginary "map" most of us carry about in our minds, an animated map that is conjured up whenever we hear the broad term, "United States."

I wonder for how many of my generation this map bears a close resemblance to those pictured in our old Tarr and Mac-Murray geography books. I am sure that for years the map that used to spring full grown into my consciousness when it was necessary for me to quickly visualize "United States" was the small outline of the country, neatly chopped off where Canada and Mexico begin, roughly divided into West, Middle West, South and East, with a few puckers for mountains, a big line for the Mississippi—and the whole thing even retaining a faint green and pink color.

A little travel, of course, does a great deal to put more life into this map. Eventually, one's job or profession is bound to color it a good deal. A politician might say that he learns to see his particular map in terms of Democrats and Republicans. An artist's map probably takes on more light and shade and at the same time has more space devoted to the human scene than most of us can visualize. I wonder if my father's personal map was largely populated with fruit trees. I wonder if the labor organizer's "United States" is marked out into organized and unorganized areas.

A map of children . . . There might be several ways to put

this together. The researcher with a geographic slant who was interested in probing into the various influences at work in molding small children might set his Arkansas pickaninny on the porch of a slanting shack in the midst of endless cotton rows. The "East" might flash into his brain as a great city of brick and concrete, with a small child playing in canyonlike streets. Quite a contrast would be the "Southwest" with the little Navajo girl spending her entire time out on the arid plain, in the shadow of high blue mountains, her summer home a shelter of juniper boughs. Then of course there would be the Southern mountain children, knowing only small cabins and the enclosed life of the wooded Appalachian slopes; children of the Northwest, who can look up daily to snow-capped peaks; children of the corn country, whose familiar "woods" are waving seas of corn; children who live beside the real seas, and grow up with that sound in their ears, that spaciousness before their eyes; children for whom spaciousness is a plain laid out like a gigantic quilt whose tufts are habitations; to say nothing of the children of our thousands of "towns," with their back-yard, house-close-to-house, main-street surroundings.

But in this kind of map, the children are more or less stationary, and the corn and the trees and the traffic do most of the moving. A psychologist's map would probably teem with the children themselves—eating, playing, obeying and disobeying, fighting, laughing, teasing; shy children and aggressive children; the maladjusted, and the happy and secure.

"But children are all alike everywhere more or less," you say. "This kind of a map of children would be a pretty uniform thing, wouldn't it? Just alive from top to bottom with little wriggling creatures?"

Whereupon the psychologist might answer that though children may very well be more alike than they are different, there *are* differences, if only in degree. Distributing children on an imaginary map is one way of getting a grasp of what the differences are, and more especially why they exist.

He would point out that down in the Southern mountains the

children of his map are going to bed without any fuss (because the whole family goes at the same time), while up North in a well regulated modern city home the battle against bedtime may go on night after night. He would point to silent Indian children in New Mexico who are content to sit for hours without playing; then contrast them with the lively little Italians hollering out on Jones Street in New York City all day, as they invent fire-escape and cardboard-carton and doorstep games.

His map would include children in school as well as at home. He would see one subdued little group in a child care center in Ohio eating lunch without a word, while the lively children in a Greenwich Village private school spin out amazing threads of conversation along with their meals. He would not be surprised to find some of these energetic, assertive children rebelling vigorously at every turn, at times throwing themselves on the floor with kicks and screams or, when thwarted, fearlessly striking out, hitting at mothers and teachers. Back in the Southern mountains again, he would expect to find more placid children, who in general seem to express much less resentment against adult authority.

In this book an attempt is made to throw into high relief one area of the psychologist's map—the Cumberland Plateau in Tennessee; to picture not only the land and the houses and other physical features, but also the way of life in this region, the standards and beliefs and hopes of the people living there. For these are responsible, on a map of children, for making the children what they are—just as on the Tarr and MacMurray relief map the lay of the land is responsible for the flow of the streams.

C. L.

New York
July, 1946

INTRODUCTION

✿✿✿✿✿✿✿✿✿✿✿✿✿✿✿✿✿✿✿✿✿✿✿✿

THIS IS A BOOK about a group of children in the Southern mountains. I am not writing about them because I think that they are
unique in every way. I have known other children much like them
in other parts of our country. In fact, I am sure that I and many
of my playmates were like them in some ways when we were children in Oregon, and my mother would probably recognize them
as even more strongly resembling the children she knew when she
was growing up in a small town in New York.

These mountain children, Scotch and English, are the sons and
daughters of men who were once coal miners and lumbermen.
Their homes are the one- or two-room cabins that their grandfathers built, still without electricity, without plumbing. Here is
one where grandmother is still the matriarch of the family. Here is
another where live not only father, mother, and seven children,
but the married daughter, her husband and baby as well. The
oldest generation remembers the days when "my precious mother
used to weave every inch of the cloth we used, and made the
thread too." Clothing comes from Sears Roebuck nowadays, but
families do still make their own quilts, kill their own hogs, and
the cycle of birth and death goes on there in the house.

Small babies are seldom out of their mothers' arms, and are
nursed whenever they cry. Often they are not weaned until they
are well along in their second year. Children are always to be seen
with their parents at buryings, at P.T.A. meetings, at square
dances. They are never left at home or put to bed early. Parents
do not seem to expect their children to live on a schedule that
differs very much from their own. Meals are the same for all members of the family, and even the youngest baby may have some of
the chocolate pie if he wants it. Children live a life very close to

that of their parents, a life involving few restrictions. Many boys and girls even drop out of school if they choose to.

However, children are taught to say "Yes'm," and are expected to obey their elders in matters that are considered important, such as behaving respectfully to grandmothers. They are whipped or threatened with whippings if they do not obey. Discipline is theoretically of the old "authoritative" kind, yet the actual routine of living is far from a strictly regulated one.

Many children are not brought up like this nowadays. In city homes it is often considered not only necessary but advisable to put the children's bedtime and mealtime on regular schedules that may be entirely different from those of the adults; to limit children's diet to the foods that are good for them though adults in the household may eat what is denied the children; to leave children at home when parents go out in the evening; and in other ways to expect the young members of the family to adhere to a special routine suitable for them.

Furthermore, many parents no longer believe in a disciplinary atmosphere that is authoritarian. They do not consider disobedience as much of a crime in their children as failure to grow in ability to control themselves.

And many of these parents have only one child. Many of them live in small apartments in the large cities. The mother works as well as the father, because she prefers to, and Ellen the maid takes Jerry out to the park to play in the afternoon.

That could not happen here in this mountain community. And of course it does not happen in many other communities in this country. Again I say these children are not unique—unless their uniqueness lies in the fact that they come from homes where the way of life and standards of behavior may be unusually representative of those that we think of as belonging specifically to our grandmothers' or great-grandmothers' childhood days. Certain elements of this way of life are still prevalent, of course, but it is not easy to find many whole communities where a good deal of the picture still hangs together as, generally speaking, it does in Summerville. It is true that modern civilization has already cut its inroads into the life of the place and is rapidly extending them. Yet here, in this clearing on the mountain top, is still to be found a generous excerpt from old times, alive and real. Until 1924 there was only a one-way horse-and-buggy dirt road up the mountain—and it was a toll road. New gadgets, new ideas, didn't travel up this road very fast, and the little population scattered in the woods on the plateau was too busy working an existence out of coal and timber—and too poor—to travel down very often.

This book is not just a description of an old-time community, however. When I came to Summerville I had no intention whatever of writing a book. I came to open a nursery school for the children of three, four, and five years of age. It was when I realized that there were marked differences between the mountain children and those with whom I had been working in Greenwich Village in New York City that I began to look more closely at the structure of the community. I wanted to find out what kind of homes and upbringing made these children so unresisting and "easy to handle." I was accustomed to the spirited ways of children whose urges to rebel were frequently strong and compelling, and whose expressions of rebellion were vigorous and fearless. And my experience had led me to expect to find among the persistent rebellers a few fundamentally troubled, "difficult" children. Why was there so little rebellion in the mountains? And was there no maladjustment among the children? What was the meaning of their outwardly peaceful, placid behavior?

And why were these children so shy for months at a time? Why was their way of playing so much less dramatic than that of the Greenwich Village children? Were they inherently less gifted in so-called "creative ability," as their accomplishments in painting, drawing, block building might seem to indicate on the surface? Was there any relation between the brilliance and talent of the New York children and their energetic, self-assertive ways? Between the mediocre performances of the mountain children and their compliant, apparently untroubled behavior?

These are the questions that prompted this study. And because

I realized that the little community of Summerville was in many respects years behind "our" times, I felt even more the urgency of making an attempt to understand its influence on the children who grew up in it. In a number of years this particular kind of living laboratory may no longer be available. New roads, and wars, are great extenders of horizons.

This book is for parents, teachers and psychologists who are faced with the problems involved in understanding children, and for all those who like to speculate on the sources of human personality and behavior.

CONTENTS

CHILDREN OF THE CUMBERLAND

THE CHILDREN IN THE HARRIET JOHNSON NURSERY SCHOOL

❀❀❀❀❀❀❀❀❀❀❀❀❀❀❀❀❀❀❀❀❀❀❀

I WAS A TEACHER in the Harriet Johnson Nursery School in New York City. Just what kind of a picture this brings to the mind of the reader I am not quite sure. For me, the memory of one little Stephen is apt to stand out particularly, more or less as a symbol of the quick imaginative insight of the brilliant children I knew that year. I see him standing at the window watching an airplane spelling out words of smoke in the sky. "That airplane is a pencil," he observes, as casually as a different kind of child might say "look."

And in the person of little David is summed up another aspect of the behavior of many of those children. But I am anticipating, jumping to the children before I have clarified the picture of the school itself.

Harriet Johnson founded, in 1919, as a part of the Bureau of Educational Experiments, the nursery school that now bears her name. She was a pioneer in this field, and undoubtedly one of the educators responsible for the fact that nursery schools are now fairly generally respected and are understood to be more than just safe places where children may come to play together and receive excellent physical care. The best of them are recognized as educational institutions and laboratories where all of the children's growing needs—physical, emotional, mental, social—are carefully studied and met as adequately as psychologist, teacher, psychiatrist, and pediatrician know how to meet them. The equipment is thoughtfully planned, certain kinds of play are particularly encouraged, and "discipline" is embodied in such an understanding, human, patient, and gentle approach on the part of the teacher that the very word, with all of its old strict connotations, is misleading.

To Harriet Johnson's influence is largely due the widely accepted concept of the primary function of the nursery school as a place where children may enlarge and clarify their experience of the real world of work and social contact, in which they are so interested. Nursery school children frequently go out with their teachers to watch the construction of a new building, visit a stable or a station or a grocery store, to find out just "how it works." The reproductions of these stables and stores, including the action that goes on inside of them, to be seen in the school later on are evidence that the new information is being digested and put to good use.

The importance of the nursery school as a situation rich in play opportunities through which children may give expression to, and thus find release from, the emotional conflicts of this stage of their growing up—an interpretation which is given a good deal of emphasis in some schools—is by no means disregarded in the Harriet Johnson Nursery School. This school recognizes both functions, and other lesser ones, in varying degrees.

But aside from the rather abstract matter of philosophy and function, just what are children in a nursery school actually doing? The visitor to the Harriet Johnson Nursery School could expect to find them vigorously and happily climbing, running, jumping; building houses and trains and boats to play in; drawing and painting and modeling; singing and skipping and dancing. But do not picture a ballet class! This roomful of children who have suddenly turned into trotting horses—and see how the idea is expressed in the play of their heads as well as their heels!—has little relation to a "dancing class." Elsewhere we find children eating at small tables and sleeping on small cots in simply furnished but bright, attractive rooms where shelves, lockers, and bathroom equipment are all scaled to the children's height and ability to reach for themselves.

The four-story concrete building that houses the Nursery

School, sandwiched in between others on a largely residential block in Greenwich Village, does not give the impression of a school to the casual observer on the outside. For where is the play yard? Sounds of children's voices floating down from the roof may finally convince him that this is, indeed, a school and no longer the Fleischman yeast factory that it once was.

The first two floors of the spacious building are devoted to the other departments of the Bureau of Educational Experiments, among them the Cooperative School for Teachers, some of whose students act as assistants in the Nursery School. As we pass by on the stairway, we have glimpses of bright walls and even of gaily painted pipes running throughout the rooms and hallways. The two upper floors, and roof, comprise the Nursery School and its offices. Here are the seven large, high-ceilinged, light rooms where the 105 children spend the major part of their day. The impression given by these rooms is a rather unusual one, from the standpoint of both cheerfulness and spaciousness. They are painted in bright yellows and greens and blues, and furnished with a minimum of clutter to allow for as much play space as possible. The only decorations are the children's own paintings hung on the walls. But in the rooms of the older groups especially, these are apt to constitute a display of startling beauty.

It is obvious that the equipment and play materials indoors and on the roof have been constructed of the best and sturdiest materials, and undoubtedly have been selected and planned down to the last detail by experts who understand the needs of children and are constantly experimenting in ways of adapting to them.

In most of the rooms are observation booths to accommodate the many visitors who seem to be as ever-present in the school as the teachers and children themselves.

And here come Stephen and David, eager to get into the picture again. After all, without them and their particular kind of play and laughter, their conversations and tears and troubles, we are talking about a meaningless, empty building. Burst open the door, Stephen and David! Come in!

Who are these two sturdy, attractive, well cared-for children, one brought to the door by his father, the other by a colored maid? Stephen is the only child in a family of actors, and David is the son of a physician whose wife also has a professional career. He, too, is an only child.

Such circumstances as these are practically duplicated in the backgrounds of most of the other children in the school, though their families scarcely could be called a homogeneous group in any simple racial, religious, or cultural sense. If there are any brothers or sisters in the family, it is seldom more than one. Frequently both parents are engaged in professional work as a matter of choice—statistics for one recent year showed that 69 per cent of the mothers worked outside of the home—making it necessary to turn the children over to maids in the after-school hours. Family incomes, ranging from $3,500 to $6,000, are usually adequate to provide for good health, though living quarters in Village apartments are anything but spacious.

A few of the children are adopted, and a few come from homes where parents are separated or have remarried, but actual count shows that the percentage of such children is probably smaller than commonly supposed—only about 12 per cent on the average.

In short, then, these are the children of a professional group living in Greenwich Village, and the fact that they are enrolled in the Harriet Johnson Nursery School usually indicates an intelligent and devoted interest in their development on the part of their parents.*

The fairly similar backgrounds of these children may account for many of the characteristics they seem to have in common. One can point to a distinct atmosphere in the school, created by the children, which varies surprisingly little from year to year. It is for this reason that I have been able to pick out Stephen and David as "symbols"—Stephen outstanding for the intelligent

* For a more detailed account of families to which this group is similar, see Caroline F. Ware, *Greenwich Village, 1920–1930* (Boston, Houghton Mifflin Co., 1935).

awareness and creative ability which so many of the children share in a marked degree, and David representing the strain and stress that seems to accompany the growing-up of not a few of these boys and girls, and to manifest itself in similar ways. That this strain and stress may be nothing abnormal under the circumstances, and nothing which is not in some degree evident in the development of all children who are free to give expression to it, may very well be the case. But at present let us concern ourselves with the "what" rather than the "why."

If we take a trip through the school, stopping in each room for a long look, spending a whole morning or even two with each group, we may be able to put our finger on the kind of behavior that makes it possible for us to speak of "the children in the Harriet Johnson Nursery School" somewhat as an entity, and to think of them in terms of "Stephen and David," remembering, of course, that there are always exceptions and that some children will have more of Stephen or David in them than other children have.

It would be well to remember, too, that what we shall be describing in the following pages are the tendencies toward various kinds of behavior apparent to a visitor in the nursery school. For our purposes we do not need to include here much of the teacher's subtle part in the picture, though certainly it must be kept in mind, especially when we see David "making trouble," that a very skillful, highly trained teacher is always there in complete control of the situation, aware of all these tendencies in her children, encouraging or discouraging them according to her understanding of the well being of the whole group and the needs of each individual.

The first room we step into may seem to be something of an exception, in the light of the foregoing remarks. These twelve babies are only two years old—some just two, some two and a half. Talking is new to them, the presence of other children is new to them, as indeed the whole of the school situation represents an unaccustomed world. They go bouncing quietly about the room, saying very little, each intent upon his own little exploration.

Yet here are the beginnings of that joy in the use of sound in language which will become very evident as we progress through the school. One little girl chants happily to herself over and over, "Mommie, Daddy, Mommie, Daddy," while another child who is playing with clay picks up the teacher's singing refrain of "Pound, pound," very easily and carries it on by himself in rhythm with his pounding movements.

And can it be that this mere baby of a boy over here is having an imaginary telephone conversation at the toy telephone? To be sure, he is. "Hello, Daddy—Hello, Daddy— Fine."

Little Michael at the table is tussling with a jig-saw puzzle, a very simple one to be sure, yet new to him and full of challenge. He keeps right at it, with no eyes for anything else that is going on in the room, and succeeds eventually in placing the pieces correctly, without help.

Assuredly there is no strain and stress apparent in this room, unless one instance—unimportant in itself, considering the ways of the two-year-old—can give us an inkling of one kind of conflict and distress which we may find more commonly in some of the older groups in the school. Donny wants the toy Peter has. He bites him on the wrist so that Peter raises a mighty wail.

In the next room, where there are fourteen children from two-and-a-half to three years old, an enormous sound is the first thing we hear, something like a song, something like a rhyme. Three little boys and girls are on a small platform,* holding to the railing and stamping their feet rhythmically with loud jumps, while they shout out, in time with their jumping, "O-Kay-O, O-Kay-O!" This seems to be a joyous game that is understood by all of the children. During the morning a number of them climb up to the platform to "O-Kay-O."

---

* A movable piece of equipment consisting of a railed platform reached by four steps.

A few others have fallen into a momentary "march" around the room, chanting nonsense syllables such as "I-lo, I-lo," out of sheer exuberance of spirit and love of sound.

Here come three, however, who are engrossed in serious conversation. They have dressed themselves up in their caps and mittens and are walking along with an air not only of being out on the street, but of being entirely grown up. "Let's go to the restaurant and eat there," says one of them.

There is a new child here today, a little boy who has never been in nursery school before. How delightedly he goes from toy to toy, from shelf to shelf, discovering all the wonders of this room where there are so many little red trucks to play with—so many little irons, and books, blocks, puzzles.

We noticed that one little girl crawled shyly and timidly off into a corner as soon as the teacher helped her off with her wraps, and has been carrying on a very intent and whispered little play with the dolls all by herself for some time.

She is not like Mary who now is out in the center of the room jumping up and down beside her block building and screaming apparently in irritation because she can't get the blocks placed to suit her. In two separate morning visits here, we notice that Mary seems to be easily and frequently upset. When she thinks another child is about to strike her, she runs screaming to the teacher for protection. She screams again, resisting the teacher's gentle suggestion that she leave her toys behind when she climbs up to the platform. And later she approaches a smaller child, intent upon whacking her on the head with a block—but the teacher prevents this and skillfully helps Mary become happily interested in her play again.

There is a little Tony, too, who seems to have his troubles. Toward the end of the morning he flings himself down on one of the small tables, kicking and screaming in a tantrum, like David himself. "No, I don't *want* these blocks. I want the *other* blocks!"

But most of the other children are deeply absorbed in their block buildings, or are contentedly washing and "ironing" the doll clothes. Here comes diminutive Isabel, bouncing out of the bathroom with a handful of dripping doll covers. She brings them up to the radiator to spread them out to dry, and does not hesitate to ask us pleasantly to move a little out of the way.

After lunch the children settle down quietly for their naps— about half of them with thumbs or fingers comfortably in their mouths—and the teacher confirms our impression that this is a lively, happy, intelligent group of Stephens and that there are only three or four really troubled Davids who tend to take a disproportionate amount of her attention.

The following day we start on the roof among the three-year-old group. We arrive early, before many of the children have come. As they enter, one by one, greeted cheerily by their teacher, they run to the apparatus, eager to slide and climb. They seem not to notice the presence of visitors at all. We are a little surprised, therefore, when one small boy almost immediately upon entering strikes out toward one of us with the little broom he is carrying—this is his greeting. And later, when we follow the group downstairs and he catches sight of us there in the room, he runs up and throws his cap at us, saying "I smack you." We watch him particularly and see that he is not just singling out the visitor. He seems to have the urge to hit the other children right and left. Indeed, we also see that the teacher is watching him particularly too, this David of hers, with one of her extra pairs of eyes as it were.

See him now, sitting with the group clustered around the student teacher who is reading a story. Every time there is a pause in the story for conversation he is annoyed and tries to hit at the child who interrupts, finally attempting to strike the student teacher too. Yet it is this same little boy, Billy, thumb frequently in mouth, who comes up to us the next day and impulsively throws his arms around us. On the whole the children seem to pay very little attention to these mild hitting gestures of his, much less than we do. "Bad boy!" they call out and go ahead with the play that is so deeply interesting and vivid and real to them.

Watch Frances kneeling beside her doll bed, talking to the doll. She is no longer Frances, but a mother, with all a mother's intonations in her voice. "Now darling, good night, good night." She tucks the doll in. A little later she runs back to the doll bed in distress. "Oh, the baby is crying!" She kneels down and "listens" to what baby is saying. "She's saying 'Da Da.' She wants her daddy!" A little boy is quickly summoned to take the part of daddy. He tucks the baby in again, plays with her for a moment, and tiptoes off. Frances goes then to the toy telephone to call the "doctor." "I didn't mean to wake you up," she apologizes, in a surprisingly realistic way.

Surprising is a good deal of the conversation and talk we hear in this room. One little girl is counting up to thirteen correctly; she is not counting actual objects, but at least she has learned to say the number series this far without a mistake. And yes, Eddie *is* counting his ten fingers correctly. This is no doubt something he has picked up at home, since there is no attempt made to teach counting to three-year-olds in the nursery school.

And here is a little fellow, just three this week, approaching a visitor with a book. He asks, with careful enunciation, "Would you kindly read me this story?" completely accepting the stranger as someone who will be friendly and helpful.

Yet later, this same little boy gets up from the dinner table with a piece of toast in his hand, walks quietly over to the visitor, saying, "I blow up on your head." But instead of blowing, he solemnly touches her on the top of the head with one finger, then goes to the student teacher and does the same thing. What intense little piece of imagination is going on in this small intellectual head? He insists, too, on having the visitor's chair for his at dessert time. "That is *my* chair for my dessert," he wails. It is a slightly larger chair than the one at his place. The exchange is made and all is happy again.

We hear bits of mealtime conversation from these three-year-olds such as, "It's the only thing we don't like (junket)." "Girls sit next to girls, boys sit next to boys." "I like Frances and you, but I don't like Polly!" "Sunday, Monday, Thursday; is after

Tuesday May?" "I'll be six." "You know how old I'll be in **July?** Seven!" "I've got a bigger toast than you, Polly." "We're too big for *his* bicycle. I'm too big for *my* bicycle. I'm a big boy. I'm taller than you!"

In this room, too, as in the last room visited, there is a good deal of happy, rhythmical "chanting." The room resounds with shouts of "Yambo Mambo!" and other wonderful rhyming sounds that unfortunately will probably never be included in any kind of dictionary of the English language. And now whole phrases and sentences appear almost in the form of songs. "We're ready today, we're ready today, woo woo woo woo woo," calls out Ruth gaily as she and Frances and Barbara begin to build a high tower of blocks. But what woe is this? Ruth is in tears now, tears of disappointment. Frances and Barbara have decided that they don't want her to play with them today after all. This is too hard to bear. Ruth screams and pulls at Barbara's hair.

Cullen is having some trouble too, but he is learning an adult technique. He and Jimmy are having a disagreement over their block building. Jimmy lifts a block as though to strike him. "No hitting!" shouts Cullen, backing off, and Jimmy does lower the block and change his tactics.

This is a day when the children go downstairs to the auditorium to play with big bouncing rubber balls. They are all eager to go, though on the way two children can't resist dashing off down the hall in the opposite direction for a brief "hide." What energy they have, these healthy Stephens, what exuberant spirits, as they never seem to tire of chasing after their bouncing balls. In fact, it is no simple feat to tell these children that the end of the period has come and it is time to stop and put away the balls. We can see that the management of this particular part of the day's routine demands a good deal of ingenuity and understanding on the part of the teacher. The majority of these children do not find it easy to stop when they are in the midst of something so delightful and satisfying to their urge for activity, even when they have had a good full period of it.

This same energetic drive is apparent in their room, where the children go eagerly from blocks to paints, to clay, to puzzles, to dramatic play in the doll corner, and almost countless other kinds of play, though never seeming to exhaust the possibilities in any of them. And their exploratory urges are constantly leading them to find new uses for old things. Jimmy at the easel not only paints a beautiful picture, but tries the paint on his hands, on the metal hinge of the easel, and experiments with changing the brushes, dripping, back and forth into opposite jars. When he suddenly perceives that their long handles are leaning across each other in the shape of an "X," the radiance and surprise that spring into his face might lead one to think that a discovery of first magnitude had just taken place—as indeed it had. This might be Stephen standing here, for a moment motionless with astonishment.

Blocks are not only played with in the middle of the room but are taken off into interesting corners, up into the shelves and cubbies, and onto the little platform. (Cullen stamps and weeps briefly when he is told that the platform has reached the limit of blocks, chairs, toys, and children that it will hold.)

Carl finds that a table is not only something to sit at, but something to try twirling himself around on. (And when the student asks him not to because it is nearly lunch time, that seems to be a signal for several more children to leap onto their tables and try the twirling, for just a few defiant moments before they heed her request. Frances calls out to the student, as she approaches, "You Dope!")

Barbara and Ruth even find new uses for their own arms and legs. They have invented a game which seems to be muscular experimentation pure and simple. They are in the doll corner, down on all fours, now and then stretching one of the "fours" high up behind them, attempting to balance on "threes."

We leave this group strongly impressed by the purposeful and constant activity of these Harriet Johnson children, by their verbal facility if not precocity, and their ability to throw themselves into their play with dramatic intensity. The urge to be "big," if not "biggest," stands out as typical, too, at this age.

That there are some conflicts among the children is perhaps

inevitable where there is so much activity. Obviously it is through these contacts and conflicts that the children are learning to build their social techniques. Conflicts with the adults are perhaps also unavoidable where the exploratory urge is so strong and where, at the same time, the relationship between children and adults is a relaxed and easy one, devoid of all elements of fear. We wonder if it is inevitable, as well, that the necessary adult "interference" should be met, in some cases, with as much resistance as is found here.

The boys and girls in the next group, where the age range is approximately from three and a half to four, are having a very happy time in the snow up here on their roof, digging, sliding, hauling. One little boy, seeing a visitor standing there in black coat and hat, calls out to her, "Black lady, will you pull us in the wagon?" with that complete fearlessness of the stranger which is characteristic of these children. ("Fearlessness," however, may not always imply a friendly acceptance! "Scram, you terrible lady," says Dorothy to this same visitor a little later. And another child, looking in her direction, dismisses her presence with, "I hate that Booger.")

Downstairs where the children are building with blocks, or cutting, modeling and painting, little Ted seems to be particularly absorbed. He has constructed two steam shovels of blocks. They are identical in every detail, and complete with derricks, dippers, and cabs that swing around. We wonder if we ourselves could build such plausible steam shovels. But watch out! One of them has crumbled! Too fragile to be pushed. Ted gets right to work again rebuilding it, with even-tempered tenacity, carefully eyeing the other one for a model.

Near him Jane encounters a little boy with a big suitcase. "Hello, Dr. Johnson," she says. "Would you like to stop and see the baby?"

"Sure!"

They go off to the doll corner and administer unto the baby, though there seems to be disagreement about which child shall be the baby. "*I* want to be the baby!"

And what do we hear down at the clay table? Sue has modeled a clay rattlesnake and is now chopping him up, making a gory little game out of it with an interested audience standing around her.

> Shall I chop him?
> One, two, ready-get-set, *chop!*
> Now shall I chop his blood out?
> One, two, ready-get-set go!
> Shall I chop his eyes out?
> One, two, ready-get-set go!
> Shall I chop his old back out?
> One, two, ready-get-set go!

Out of curiosity we ask the teacher if there are any children in this group—any Davids—who have real difficulty getting through the days peacefully and happily. To our surprise, the answer is "Yes, about four." What we have seen in the room might lead us to suppose that there were no difficulties, or at least that they had been largely redirected into constructive channels.

But we do get an idea of what the teacher must mean when we see two little boys at the easel. One has covered his whole sheet with glorious bright red. How he loves it! He begins to splatter it on the table near by. The student teacher comes up to remind him to keep the paint on the paper, and he daubs it on her white cuffs, recklessly hitting at her with his brush, to ward her off. Needless to say, he is not allowed to continue this procedure. This is the same little boy who has such fun with a "pal" during the morning, in a slightly silly way. They make funny faces at each other and talk in funny tones of voice, laughing excitedly.

And Dorothy is suddenly hitting, biting, and spitting at the student who has approached her with an apparently unacceptable suggestion.

But now music time has come and all troubles vanish. The

children sit with their teacher in a circle on the floor and sing together. A few even ask to sing their own original songs, songs about boats and airplanes. With complete unself-consciousness these "songs" come out clear and strong and full of tunefulness.

With the same interest and attention the children gather about their teacher for a story. When she tells them that the little boy in the story is four years old, we hear a chorus of "He's as old as me!" "I'll be four and a half in the summer!"

On the following day the children have a rhythms period. This means a trip in the elevator down to the auditorium on the first floor, and on this day it happens to mean an extra long wait on the bench outside the room. Another group inside is slow in coming out. Waiting is hard. The teacher knows this and in a really delightful way plays singing games with the children, so that they do not have to try to just wait quietly with nothing to do. The majority of the children obviously love these games, but for Benny it is too long to sit. He dashes off down the hall, and two more follow him. They ignore or resist the student teacher's efforts to bring them back. Now a few more of them are off, racing and jumping up and down the hall. "You Dope!" shouts Wally to the teacher, striking at her, when she prevents him from joining the others. To be sure, they all *do* come back after their little fling. They do not defy their loved teacher to the same degree that they do the student assistant.

Here in rhythms these active, dramatic, imaginative children, these Stephens, are in their element. They play that they are snowflakes, "gently falling down." Their concentration, translated into beautiful body movement, is a wonderful thing to behold.

"Time to go" is as hard as "have to wait," for these children just as for those in the three-year-old group. There is a little resistant dashing about and hiding in corners before all can be brought to the door to line up for the trip upstairs to lunch.

At the lunch table Paul announces, "I'm thinking of something that goes around very fast!"

Dorothy: "Is it an airplane propeller?"

Paul: "No!"

Ted: "Is it a merry-go-round?"

Paul: "No! It's an electric fan!"

During this lunch period we notice something that has not been very evident in the other groups as yet. We have heard "Dope" before, but now another favorite word crops out. "You will not, Dope. You will not, Stink."

And again, referring to the student teacher, "Miss Foster is Stinkie." In fact, later on, when one of these children asks a visiting adult her name, his response when told is, "Oh, Miss Stinkie."

Just pure nonsense, shouted at the top of the lungs, appears at this lunch time too. "Miss Foster's made of toast!" "Miss Stankie-Poo!"

Some of the unwanted food is slung on the floor by the master builder of steam shovels, who also seems to have a predilection for upsetting his table (when there are no dishes on it, of course!).

The teacher reestablishes calm and gets the children's minds again on more "sensible" conversation. We understand now what she means by her "difficulties." The urge to resist adult control and to resist the "musts" in the routine of the day is as strong among many of these children as it was in the group last visited.

But seeing the teacher's skill in rechanneling these drives, we understand why they are not always apparent.

When we enter the four-year-old room, we are so caught up in a maelstrom of activity, of resounding voices, that we scarcely know which way to look. A little girl enters on all fours. "Good-by, Rover," her mother calls out gaily as she leaves.

The floor in this room appears to have been converted into a huge airport. The airplanes, made of blocks, are intricately and thoughtfully constructed. Their owners push them about with slow care, so they will not break, and we hear bits of talk about "R.A.F." and "navy bombers." "Mine's better than yours," one challenges another. "No, mine's better than *yours*," the other retorts, and proves it by a masterpiece of imagination. "You know what mine's called? The—(hesitating, then booming and mouthing it out authoritatively), *The Stankie-Bansom,* that's what it's called!"

But what is the trouble?—a little boy in tears, over here at the "train" (row of chairs).

"He wants to go to New Haven, and this train doesn't go to New Haven. It goes to Miami."

"And Florida," supplies another little boy.

"Miami *is* Florida," the first little boy corrects disdainfully.

The difficulty seems to evaporate in a moment's time. All three boys are on the train now, chugging away to Florida—or is it New Haven?

And is this baby talk we hear? Dora is lying on a cot playing baby. She has selected another little girl to be her nurse. "Tick-a-tick-a-ta," she coos, and reaches out playfully to the nurse.

Yet there is really nothing babylike about this little girl. She likes to talk so much and so fast, as indeed do most of the others, that the teacher makes slow progress with the story at story time. "Shut up, I want to talk," Dora finally calls in exasperation, eager to give her description of a penguin. "They look a little like ducks but they're not, they're penguins, one foot up and one foot down."

Here comes Sammy from the carpenter shop, zooming across the room with the "derrick" he has just made. "Show me where the broken pipe is! I'm the man who fixes it!"

Carl, a very professorial looking little fellow, emerges from the shop with something he labels a "mechanical piston rod."

Little Julie seems to be clinging close to the teacher all the while, not playing with the other children, constantly calling for the teacher's attention in a mournful drawl. When she accidentally knocks a wing off another child's airplane he calls her "Dope!" and she runs crying to the teacher. "I'm *not* a Dope, am I?"

In fact, being called "Dopey" is a form of teasing that is particularly distressing to these children. "I'm *not* a Dope!" is a vigorous denial we frequently hear, with the accompaniment of tears or screams or other manifestations of real woe. Nor do the student teachers escape the epithet in this group. "Go away, Dopey," shouts Joey when the student makes a suggestion about moving his building to a better place.

Now there are screams and tears again. This seems to be the reaction typical of these four-year-olds when there are threats to rights or property or person; no less than fourteen instances of this sort occur in one morning. Yet, also typically, these difficulties are very short-lived, and two who were screeching and pulling at each other's hair one moment are happily playing together the next. "It is, *too*, nice!" screams and stamps Beverley, when Jerry claims that her block building is not a good one.

The next moment all troubles are forgotten while Jerry urgently calls the hospital on the telephone: "Hospital, hospital! My turtle is sick and I want you to come here very quick!" The ambulance comes and takes the turtle to the hospital. This is very serious play. Many of the children have gathered around to watch and take part. "Here doctor, here doctor! A hurt turtle! I put a bandage on her foot and she'll have to stay in the hospital two weeks!"

The ambulance brushes against one of the airplanes and displaces a block. Jerry quickly puts the block back where it belongs. "I didn't mean to, Sammy," he explains with genuine consideration.

But Joey sits calmly at the table, paying no attention to all of this play. Much of the time he is sucking his thumb while intent upon the picture he is coloring. Can it be that this is an *ant-eater* he is drawing? Yes, it is "a baby ant-eater, and I'm making it for you, Sally." More and more wonderful creatures appear from the point of this little boy's crayon—a realistic turkey, weasels, and ships steaming along.

Sally is a little girl who has been sucking two fingers much of the morning herself, with the other hand holding a small piece of cloth up near her mouth, under her nostrils. Suzanne also sucks her fingers practically the whole morning as she plays, sometimes pulling her wooly collar up to her mouth along with her fingers.

Several children are modeling with clay now—blimps, "gyros," cookies, sugar bowls, turtles. Joey has made a really wonderful snail. "Isn't this a good snail?" he says, holding it up for all to see. "Gooder than anybody's; gooder than Jerry's, gooder than . . . ," but his thumb pops back into his mouth and he doesn't finish the catalog—audibly, that is.

At lunch time the children delight in helping pass the food and insisting on the use of the prearranged "signals." "Quiet signal! Quiet signal!" booms Dora, as she marches around solemnly with the plate of toast.

The intellectual little creator of weasels and snails resorts for a moment to nonsense with a new element in it, while he is eating.

"That's a pee-pee, isn't it?"

"No, that's a big slopper piece of toast."

When the children go up to their roof in the afternoon, several of them, who must have been to the Central Park Zoo, play seal. Their "barking" is so realistic that one almost looks around for a live seal. Sam seal gives Jamie seal a playful bite in the hair—perhaps pulling a little of it out—as they flop about close together. Jamie is somewhat concerned for a minute, not knowing quite what to make of this bite, which may have been a harder one than intended. He rubs his head briefly, then with a twinkle says—and this might be the real Stephen speaking— "Oh well, I needed a haircut anyway!"

On the junglegym are perched two little boys who are, for the moment at least, defying the world. They look down at their teacher and plan together excitedly like big tough guys, "Let's hit her on the head. Let's put her in jail. Put her in a fire!"

Nor must we forget the rhythmic chanting that is to be heard among the children here as elsewhere throughout the school. "Mr. My-Gate, Mr. My-Gate" is a funny little shout three boys make up for their own accompaniment as they march around together. And indeed, Jerry is practically singing his sentences the whole morning long.

Activity, activity—purposeful, happy, social activity that is bound to have its accompaniment of momentary tears and troubles, as well as its instances of cooperation and sympathy—but always activity and voices, voices.

The floor in the five-year-old room is covered with elaborate block buildings, and at a glance we can see that the play going on is highly developed and accurate in detail. No longer are turtles being taken to the hospital! Here are train tracks with the power lines beside them. Here are laundries, jails, boats, beautiful houses which are masterpieces in architectural balance and form, and more tracks with automobile crossings carefully guarded by gates.

We hear, "Inspect the tracks.". . . "It's a kind of switch turntable.". . . "If he wants to talk to one of these inspecting cars he goes down the ramp."

These children seem to have learned to get along without screaming and jumping at each other. That their room could be called "quiet" is not the case; it fairly reverberates with the loud noise of many eager voices all talking at once. But there is no sound of friction.

Little Eric seems to have a tendency to go off into silly, somewhat chaotic behavior that sets off the others too. As he enters now, three or four of the children start wagging their heads at him and saying "Boo-boo, Boo-boo!" He responds with a series of quick "Bangs!" and silly gestures. At unpredictable times during the morning he seems to lapse into this need to "bang" about aimlessly for a few minutes, an indication of immaturity of which one would not otherwise be aware.

In fact, most of these children with their splendid fund of information and their ability to settle arguments by appealing calmly to the teacher or by "talking it out," seem so mature and look so large and well developed physically that it is a little startling to see five of them with thumbs in their mouths at the story time. One little fellow—or should I say big fellow?—twists a strand of hair on his head with one hand while he sucks the thumb of the other hand. This he does most of the morning, not only at story time.

In this room, "chanting" has become real singing. As we leave, one little girl bursts spontaneously into "The First Noel." This must be a favorite, loved song. Others join in at once. For a moment the talking voices are still. The room is filled with the sound of singing.

Can we sum up in a sentence what we mean by "the children in the Harriet Johnson Nursery School?"

Perhaps first of all we think of them as beautifully robust, healthy children with sturdy bodies. Almost simultaneously we think of them as very vocal children. They talk clearly, constantly, copiously, with a facility and pace that is paralleled only by their muscular activity in general. Harriet Johnson children seem never still for long. They must be running, rushing, hopping, jumping, twisting, turning, most of the time. Perhaps the screaming which we think of as the characteristic way in which many of the children react to troubles, and the easily aroused tendency toward excitement, are but other aspects of this same urge to activity. Indeed, the very troubles that arise among the children are hardly to be separated from the idea of social activity and the working out of social techniques through this activity. Nor can they be separated from the picture of intensity with which these children approach every part of their world. They are intense in their play, their anger, their enthusiasms.

That these are gifted children of a high level of intelligence is evident even without the IQ scores to corroborate the fact. Their awareness is keen, their curiosity in the world about them eager and strong. And the creative skills of these Stephens, apparent in their intricate and beautifully designed block buildings, their ingenious drawings, their highly expressive movements in rhythms, their imaginative language—these do not distinguish just one or two artistic children, but are the means of expression habitual to most of them, as natural to them as walking and talking.

And, should I add, as natural as the urge to resist and rebel and assert oneself which seems characteristic of many of the children? That this urge is stronger in some than in others is true, yet it is one of the unmistakable ingredients in the "atmosphere" of the Harriet Johnson Nursery School. Particularly among those who defy adult control are found the few real Davids, the not entirely happily adjusted children who make themselves known by their exaggerated need to strike out and destroy, either verbally or actually, or conversely by their fearful cringing and withdrawal.

Occasionally it happens as a matter of chance—certainly not very often—that the proportion of children in one group who require an especially careful and understanding approach on the part of the teacher is greater than just three or four. My year of teaching was one of these years. Half of the fifteen four-year-olds were full-fledged Davids as well as Stephens. Though this meant that our room was brilliant with paintings of remarkable beauty, and was alive with the constructive activity of children whose keen minds were busy exploring their new world, it also meant that our days were apt to be punctuated with temper tantrums, tears and fights and screams, wetting as well as the refusal to go to the bathroom, destruction of children's block buildings, chaotic, silly play, excitement over "tough" talk of chopping down the school and throwing the teacher out of the window, as well as "bathroom talk," and always pugnacious resistance to every "must."

Needless to say, teaching such children is something of a strenuous adventure in ingenuity and patience, a vigorous exercise in skill of understanding, in ability to turn what might be chaos into something more calm. The rebels must be helped through their rebellion. Destructiveness, when it goes out of healthy bounds, must be channeled into constructiveness through the vital and interesting play opportunities, materials, and ideas presented to the children, as well as through the warm, solid, bolstering relation of friendliness and understanding that is established with them.

When June came I left this most challenging and stimulating situation to start a play group for the mountain children at the Highlander Folk School in Tennessee. I did not know a great deal about the South and its people and had very little idea of what to expect in the summer that lay ahead of me.

THE CHILDREN IN THE SUMMERVILLE
NURSERY SCHOOL

✿✿✿✿✿✿✿✿✿✿✿✿✿✿✿✿✿✿✿✿✿✿

FROM A MODERN, fireproof concrete building on a crowded city street to a small wooden shack once used for an Episcopal mission and with a crude "altar" still there against the wall; from a paved playground on the roof with its pebble pits and junglegyms to an unfenced meadow where apple trees grew; from up-to-date equipment to a handful of boxes and boards for playthings and an outhouse for sanitation; from healthy, immaculately clean children in bright corduroy overalls to barefoot boys and girls in "real" Sears Roebuck overalls, boys and girls whose first teeth were sometimes rotting out, whose arms and legs were frequently covered with sores, whose noses commonly were running with chronic colds; from David and Stephen to—what?

These Johnnie Mays and Ella Carolines, Paul Williams and J.W.'s who came to my summer nursery school were three, four, and five years old. To most of them, a nursery school was a completely new situation. They were used to playing with their many brothers and sisters, but not with a large group of other children. Their homes were more or less scattered in the woods and clearings of the mountain community known as Summerville, located in what was once a coal mining and timber area, at this time abandoned by everything but the W.P.A.

When I think back to that month of July spent out in the meadow with those twelve or fifteen children and try to find a way to characterize the "atmosphere" of this little Summerville nursery school, the two words that seem inevitably right are "inactivity" and "silence."

Here they are—twelve of them on this hot day. The morning is already one hour gone, but the children are mostly sitting silently on the grass or in the sand pile, and some of them are just standing, watching. Horace seems frozen to the spot where his big sister left him. But who is this bustling around with some show of activity? Only the teacher, trying with all her might to interest the children in playing train with this old bench, or in building houses out of the orange crates.

Now it is time to go inside for a mid-morning lunch, eagerly eaten by all except the newest comers, who are too shy to touch it. The teacher tries to read a story, but blankness reigns on the faces of most of the children. Let's try a song then. How about a hammer song, pounding while we sing? The song turns out to be the teacher's solo. Not a hand is lifted to pound along with hers. How about playing train? Let's chug along just like the train that passed by this morning. There is one volunteer; all the others sit solemnly and watch.

When we go back outdoors, there is a little more activity than during the first hour. More of the children are playing, more of them talking a little (yet teacher is at her wit's end to understand much of this talk: "Nit Wooey, shee nit buh puhnin' thih," says one little four-year-old, meaning "Miss Lewis, see this bus pulling this"). Three-year-old Clarence is hammering away with the skill of a seven-year-old, making an orange crate chair. Here is George actually roughly pushing another child out of the swing; yes, he is one boy who may turn out to be a David. And here is Paul William chatting happily and fearlessly without a trace of shyness as he decides to go blackberry picking; while John busily constructs an excellent airplane out of the boxes and boards.

But Elsie May stands silently and tensely by herself, when she must relinquish the loved swing to someone else; little three-year-old J.B. still dogs every step of his older brother and cries quietly to himself much of the time—a more unhappy and mournful little face I never did see.

What has become of the maelstrom of voices and activity? Where is the screaming to which I am accustomed, and also the happy chanting? Aren't these children ever going to get "wild," silly, excited, as has been a tendency in almost every other group of children I have known? Are they always going to accept this school routine so placidly, with so little resistance or rebellion? Will they in time develop more of a love for stories, singing, skipping, dancing? These are the questions I asked myself as I looked around at some of the timid faces and realized that I scarcely knew the sound of the voices that went with them.

I left after a month, returning in the fall to open the nursery school on a permanent basis. I said to myself, these are very shy children. No doubt it is just taking them a long time to "loosen up." And possibly the humid summer heat has had something to do with their passivity— "So hot it makes you feel like a lizard out on a log, pantin' for breath!" as one mountain man put it. Surely more of both David and Stephen will become apparent as time goes on.

At the end of two and a half years, it was true that the picture had changed really a good deal. All of the children who had been in the school from the start had become much more noisy; one or two presented real problems akin to David's; most of them had gradually developed more of Stephen's abilities; yet for all this, they remained to the end, Johnnie May and J.W. Even after the loosening influence of years it was difficult to take a visitor to see them. They were still the shy children of shy mountain people, and in the presence of the outlander they were apt to shrink and freeze and lose all spontaneity. Indeed, it was seven months before little three-year-old Anna could bring herself to talk even to me, her teacher. And Evelyn, who was six, brought water from home in a jar, rather than have to ask me for a drink at school. A strange visitor remained always someone to peek at shyly from around the corner of the house or from a tight shell of reserve quickly drawn on over one's clothes, if no corner was handy.

It is easy enough, however, to look at these children from the safe distance of the printed page. Here we can listen to them, watch their play, and try to discover just what it is that makes J.W. on his mountain top essentially somewhat different from David on his roof top, in spite of the fact that they are both children living in these United States.

Here we are on a warm spring day, out in the back yard of our school—no longer the Episcopal mission house but another quite similar cabin near by. This house does not stand in a meadow, but is set back in the woods. Pine trees and young oaks and the spreading leaves of the wild grapevines arch over our fenced-in yard and keep us in the welcome shade.

Here are trees for climbing, boards propped up against the fence for running up and down; a see-saw made out of a huge rolling log; and swings of various sorts, to say nothing of quite an assortment of boxes, barrels, tires, tin dishes, toy trucks, shovels, and odds and ends such a broken clocks and remains of old kerosene stoves.

But a number of the children are just standing around or sitting watching, as was the case in the early days of the school. Julia has been there on the steps for twenty minutes, sucking her thumb, content to wait idly for her turn in the swing. Edward has rolled a tire around the house several times, but now is lying in it curled up, resting. He looks tired this morning, as he often does.

Of course, other children are busy playing—riding the tricycle, pulling the wagon around the house, swinging, digging and loading the little trucks with "coal." Three of the older ones have organized a playhouse group. Ernestine goes off to find leaves for "poke salad," while Ella Caroline and Marvin just sit in the playhouse and chat as they wait for her return.

Martin and Billy, stalking along with their pointed sticks over there in the high weeds, are out "huntin' rabbits." Buddy and Horace are nowhere to be seen, but we can hear them clearly. They have retired to the floor of the back porch where they play marbles for hours on end in the springtime. Buddy supplies a running commentary replete with all the schoolboy marble idioms: "We're goin' to start over again, ain't we? Oh! I knocked one! I knocked old daddy off the top! Now Horace, it's your shot. . . . Horace, let me put these back in. Let me shoot with your tall ones and you shoot with my tall ones, see? Let's swap tall ones . . . Aw, he winned that one, didn't you, Horace? I guess I ain't got but two more. Now put 'em up together. I'm gonna win some off of Horace. These big ole log rollers are knockin' 'em in a line!"

Yes, there is activity, but it impresses one more as a placid sort of activity, rather than that zooming, surging urge at the Harriet Johnson Nursery School.

When the older boys and girls go off with the student helper—a girl from the neighborhood who is paid by the N.Y.A.—to look for frog's eggs down at the "branch," the littler ones, finding themselves masters of the whole place, stop sucking their thumbs and liven up considerably. But even so, here is Barbara contentedly playing alone; here is Anna not speaking a word as she busily puts her doll to bed in Virginia's house; here are three little girls just sitting together in the shade looking at picture books and talking to themselves about the pictures: "Thar's the little pony with his mamma. Looka thar! Thar he goes with a mushroom, gallopin' off with it in his mouth. That little pony run and found his mamma. He was a-comin' right through some weeds, wasn't he, and she was plowin' in the ground. They're goin' to get off thar and drink 'em some water."

When these little girls are through with the books, they will go in and get their crayons and bring them out to the table under the grapevine where they will sit and draw and chat tirelessly for the remaining half of the morning.

Placid, but very pleasant, not lacking in fun and gaiety of a kind. Someone calls out to J.B. to come and ride in the wagon. J.B. is pumping himself high in the swing. Wiry, sure-footed (is there a tree around his house up which he has not "shinnied"?), he is a past master at pumping. "Why, I *am* ridin'," he calls out merrily. "I'm ridin' myself. What's a matter, can't you see me?"

Martin, while he was out "rabbit huntin'," found a long stick that makes a good horse, a very spirited beast, in fact. Here he comes astride it, charging and prancing and puffing and shouting the kind of jargon the mountain men use with their horses: "Come up here! Come around here! Get up now, and I'll turn ye out in a minute. Come up here! Whoa! Come up here! Whey, Luther Bell, Whey, Luther! Whey, Luther! Yea cross, Yea cross, Yea cross! Old horse is tryin' to get away. He kin go faster than a cowboy's horse."

At this, J.B., still from his perch in the swing, observes in his mischievous, superior five-year-old vein, "Shoot, you can't ride on a piece of wood!"

Ella Caroline sings to herself, while she sweeps out her play-house, a song she has learned from her daddy—

> Oh little water boy,
> Bring your water around,
> If you don't like your job,
> Set your water bucket down.

And Wayne Edward, with his twinkle that is much like Stephen's, tirelessly calls to me, over and over, "Miss Lewis?" I supply the wanted answer, "What?" "Chickens squawk, that's what!" he retorts triumphantly, proud of the acquisition of this little trick which is a game popular among school children in the community.

But all of this pleasantness and comparative inactivity do not mean that there is never any *noise*. If this were a rainy day and all twelve of these children, young and old, were playing in the small room indoors, the clatter and clamor of this play might even send the visitor scuttling out at once. There is much chugging along of trucks and banging them up in dire accidents, accompanied by the constant calling from all directions of "Mim Moois, Wook!" or simply "Un-huh, Mit Sewis, un-huh!"—a common expression which seems to mean, "Look, see what I have to show you!" In one corner some of the little girls are rocking their dolls to sleep to the lusty singing accompaniment of "It's the old time religion, the old time religion," rasped out in true mountain style (that means with a nasal, slurring twang). The pounding of hammers coming from the small adjoining kitchen, converted into a tem-porary carpenter shop, doesn't help the situation any.

Noise, yes, especially when the lively five-year-old boys who have been in the school for two years are present. Three of them on this rainy day are running the small trucks on roads they have constructed of blocks. One says nothing as he plays, but the other two keep up a steady stream of both conversation and monologue: "This old road is so rough I got stuck on it." "I got stuck up too." "By gosh, I had a wreck!"

But still this is not quite the same thing as Harriet Johnson "noise," chiefly because of the almost total absence of screaming.

What, is it possible that these Tennessee mountain children do not get into fights and grabs and tiffs? Oh, indeed they do fight and hit and pull for what they want, when necessary, but apparently without any need to resort to screeching as a result or accompaniment, even after they have lost their shyness. Look at Martin and Wayne Edward, boys of four and five years old. They are going fiercely at each other, probably over whose turn it is to play with the coveted red truck—turbulent Martin is one child, the only child, who is quick to strike out in rage, defending himself against what he seems to expect will be constant encroachments. But now the boys stop as suddenly as they started. Glaring and speechless they rise, and just walk off. And later in the day, when we are lined up for cod liver oil, Buddy, infuriated, suddenly gives Wayne Edward a terrific smash in the face. "I told you to stop pinching me!" he shouts with authority. Wayne Edward is abashed, and must be somewhat hurt, but is determined not to show it. He smiles weakly and changes the subject.

Now Wayne Edward's little three-year-old sister is in trouble and has burst into tears. "J.B. hit me." "Well, *she* hit me." The whole matter seems to settle itself when Wayne Edward thereupon marches over and deliberately hits J.B.'s little sister, Anna, and comes and reports it to me, seeming to reason that "if he hits my sister I'll make it even by hitting his!" Little Anna, by the way, just looks on rather bewildered by it all, not even crying.

Other children, when they get "hit," are apt to dissolve into very silent tears, seeking no attention for them. Such a child is Ernestine. I suddenly find her weeping quietly while I am reading a story to the group sitting around me. She tells me that "Richard hit me," but I can get no further comment out of either of them.

Quickly come, quickly gone are these difficulties, apparently without the accompaniment of much strain, and in fact days and days go by without any tears and troubles at all, except in the summer when tender bare feet are easily hurt. And indeed, many of the fights, especially among children new in the school, seem to evaporate when I no more than look (not at all fiercely!) in the direction of the combatants, so aware are these children of adult approval or disapproval.

However, there was frail little four-year-old Annie Pearl who *did* scream, loudly and furiously, when she got into difficulties with her favorite playmate, who was also a constant companion at home, since the two were neighbors. They would both snatch and grab for the same plaything relentlessly, Virginia maintaining a firm silence, but Annie Pearl screeching just like a New Yorker. This came in the midst of the summer heat, when tiny little Annie Pearl seemed very irritable, hating to be touched. The first time I heard the screaming it struck me as something so unusual, coming from one of these mountain children, especially one who had just started to school, that I straightway made a special section in my notes for "Annie Pearl's screaming." But winter came along, Annie Pearl stayed home from school unwell, and when she returned the following spring the screaming never seemed to happen any more.

For a three-week period during that spring I kept careful count of all instances of tears, screams (if any!), hits, or fights among the children that might be called "disturbances of the peace," exclusive of conflicts with adults (which were almost never in the picture) and tears due to physical hurt. Seven was the maximum for one morning, among eleven children, ages three to five. On no other day did so many occur. Compare this with twenty in one morning in the four-year-old group of thirteen children at the Harriet Johnson Nursery School, on a day considered by the teacher a comparatively peaceful one.

Whether or not it has any connection with screaming, it is also true that these Johnnie Mays and J.W.'s have much less verbal facility, even after two and a half years, than David and Stephen. Their talking is certainly neither constant, clear, nor copious. I have indicated the kind of delayed "baby talk" that is characteristic of many of them, even when they are as old as five. Not that every child speaks in this manner; little Barbara talked as clearly as an adult at the age of two and a half. But I could usually count on being able to understand readily only about half of the children in the group, in spite of the fact that older children graduated and new ones kept coming into the school. "Bial won' kay on it," says five-year-old Marvin, referring to a bridle staying on. Is he imitating the boy next door who can't speak clearly because of a cleft palate? "Gars beel!" calls out four-year-old Emma Doris, who did not start to talk at all till she was three. (This "Gars beel" may possibly mean "Giddap Bill.") When she says "Hi go wass um" as she loads her wagon, I really do not know what she means. But more intelligible is "Hi, hi gah me a witta bitty mail bush, a witta tuck too." (Emma Doris's mouth hangs open much of the time, with tongue protruding. No doubt her tonsils need attention.)

But aside from this matter of pronunciation, the vocabularies of the Summerville children cannot compare with those of the Harriet Johnson children. "Mechanical piston rods," "ramps," "roundhouses," "penguins," are things that a Cumberland mountain child knows very little about—and probably his dad knows almost as little.

Moreover, the mountain child's grammar sometimes follows its own peculiar laws. The common expression, "Aw, it ain't done it!" (meaning "It isn't so!") undergoes unexpected metamorphoses and becomes "Aw, I am done it!" or "It *is* done it!" Ina Lee says to Edna, "You ain't got a clean dress to wear to Sunday School!" Edna's retort is, "Aw, I *have* done it!"

And as I have already indicated, the spoken word is entirely locked up in many of these children until the wall of shyness breaks down. A few children started to school without any of this reserve at all, chirping merrily from the first day, but most of them talked very little at first, taking weeks or even months to loosen up. "I am only just now beginning to be aware of so-and-so's voice," was a frequent comment in my notes.

And though the children who are no longer shy love to sing all during the day the ballads and hymns they hear so frequently at home, yet the rhythmic chanting which is one of the most striking characteristics of the Harriet Johnson children is scarcely ever in evidence here—as though that were a special kind of language, a foreign language, unknown to Summerville children. Any instances of this sort must be described in terms of *"Once* I heard Ernestine (five and a half years old) pushing the train and chanting 'choo choo CHOO, I haul, haul, HAUL,' " or *"One day* Ella Caroline (five and a half) made up a little chant of 'ain't no count, ain't no count.' " But as for all the delightful nonsense of O-Kay-O and I-Lo from the younger children—no, words and sounds do not come from them in that way.

It is interesting in this connection that most of the ten children who took the Stanford-Binet intelligence tests fell down noticeably on questions requiring a verbal formulation of an answer, or even verbal repetition of a sentence, probably partly because of unfamiliarity with some of the vocabulary, partly because of lack of skill in manipulating words, as well as self-consciousness. After the examiner asked little four-year-old Julia to repeat, "Tom has lots of fun playing ball with his sister," she simply asked, with candor and some bewilderment, "What is 'Tom'?" and could not be induced to attempt the sentence. Lack of native intelligence could scarcely have been a factor in explaining the children's failures on such questions. Most of their scores fell within the range of normal, two a little below, one slightly above, verbal difficulties notwithstanding.

But perhaps it is time to stop picturing the children as they "are" and consider them more as they "have been" during this two-and-a-half-year period, what tendencies cropped up, what phases of behavior appeared and disappeared. It is a mistake to think of children as static personalities, when indeed they shed their traits and take on new ones as easily and almost as predictably as trees shed leaves in autumn and sprout new ones in the spring.

It was noticeable that the mountain children were not under the same compulsion to consider themselves "big" and "biggest" and "taller than you" and "best in the world" and "old" that was so common among the Harriet Johnson children. In fact, many of them were scarcely age-conscious at all. On Edward's fourth birthday I thought that it would be pleasant to sing Happy Birthday to him in school, but to my surprise he did not even know that it was his birthday and could not tell me how old he was. Indeed, it was not unusual to find much older children in the community who did not know their ages, and even parents who could not tell me the birth dates of some of their children without looking up the record in the trunk.

But these mountain children, though they would scarcely know what it meant to look forward to being "four and a half" and seldom referred to themselves as "big," *did* love to be *first*, first in any line, whether it was for washing or even for cod liver oil!

As might be expected, the tendency toward excited giggling and "silly," chaotic nonsense play in this group of children was very slow in developing. Months passed before there was any very noticeable trace of it. And when it finally did begin to crop up now and then, it was largely among the four- and five-year-old boys who had been in the school from the beginning, and no longer found the play materials so full of interest.

Occasionally, too, a new child— I think of Junior who was five and a half—used silly faces and giggles as a way of making his first contacts with the other children in the school, not unlike the little boy in the upper group of three-year-olds at the Harriet Johnson Nursery School.

I was somewhat perplexed by an excited laugh that seemed to be the only way in which one or two of our children could laugh, as though laughter had been pent up and now was coming out all in a burst, not quite knowing what to make of itself. One of these children was our most serious, sensitive, observant little boy, five years old at the time. He was very close to the business of living, and would frequently carry on with me such conversations as the following:

Buddy: "Why don't you get some more of these blocks for us, Miss Lewis?"

Me: "I haven't the money, I'm sorry to say."

Buddy: "Why don't you get the money?"

Me: "How would I?"

Buddy: "Work for it."

Me: "But I have to come here and teach you. How could I work for money?"

Buddy: "Work here teaching us."

Yet for a period of several months Buddy could not seem to laugh over anything in a way that was not tinged with excitement, with a quality of being somewhat beside himself, which indeed was evident in many of the children (and perhaps I should add is common to children everywhere) whenever we did anything together that was a very unusual experience for them. I remember that beautiful day in December when I took six of the older ones off into the woods to hunt for holly. We took our graham crackers along and made a picnic of it. This kind of outing was so new to them, and such fun, that they chattered and rushed along in an excited, keyed-up state I had never seen them in before.

And the night at the Folk School when community children of all ages were invited over to see themselves in colored slides on the screen, they found this such an unaccustomed sight, and also apparently so embarrassing, that the only response was a chorus of screams, squeals, almost hysterical in quality, with some of the children shouting, "Take it off! Take it off!" when they saw their own pictures.

But "silliness" as a teacher sometimes knows it and has to cope with it, hysterical giggling that occurs day after day in such a prolonged way as to interfere with constructive work, was scarcely ever a problem. On the whole, however, it was not so easy to keep the Tennessee children "constructively" occupied as it was the Harriet Johnson children.

I have already mentioned that some of the boys began to tire of our play materials. The possibilities inherent in a set of blocks, for instance, seemed to be much less for J.W. than for Stephen. Day after day Stephen could convert the blocks into boats, trains, stables, houses, laundries, theatres, bakeries, stores—not merely as a block-building exercise, though undoubtedly he must have derived much satisfaction from these tangible evidences of his ability to put form and balance and beauty into a mass of plain blocks, but this was his way of learning more about the busy world about him, of digesting and mastering the fund of information he was storing up.

For J.W., however, there seemed to be no such potentialities in blocks. Was it because his world was not so full of innumerable intriguing places such as bakeries and docks and fire stations for him to explore? places that lend themselves very well to reproduction in block form?

Time and again I sat down and thought, "What can I provide for J.W. at the nursery school that will help him have a more constructive, expansive sort of day? How can I both stimulate his curiosity and help him satisfy it? Is there any way in which I can make this nursery school more than a place to come for jumping and swinging and good food and contact with other children? Can I help him make his playing a thing that is more rich in *content?*" To fill the day "well" came to be quite a challenge, in the case of the older children, even though I made considerable departure from the concept of "well" that I had held at the Harriet Johnson Nursery School.

It was noticeable that these mountain children rarely threw themselves into their play with the complete immersion that the Harriet Johnson children did. Ina Lee, while she rocked her doll, remained Ina Lee. She did not lose her identity in a mother-role and assume a mother's tone of voice. Nor did the little boys use the gruff tones of men as they dug and hauled and unloaded coal. And certainly "baby talk" put on for fun would be an anomaly.

Let us look more closely at this play. Ella Caroline has organized a playhouse group under the twisting grapevine. Barbara, who is one of the smaller children, has been corralled to take the part of the baby—almost never is this part taken by an older child, as Dora took it in New York. But wait a moment—Barbara is in tears. She has stubbed her bare toe. Who is this galloping around from the other side of the house at the sound of her sobs? Her five-year-old brother and protector. "Who hurt Barbara?" he roars, ready to avenge with a good wallop if necessary. When he is satisfied that no one has hurt her, he goes back to his digging with the older boys and Barbara submits to being "washed" as the baby of the house.

When these mountain girls and boys play house, they do not call the doctor for sick babies. Instead we hear such snatches as, "I'm makin' up bread. Ain't dis a mess o' dough!" "Don't get the eggs, let 'em set!" "We ain't fixin' to move." "Are you gettin' you'uns a hog?" "I'm goin' to turn in and wash all these sure-enough dishes." "I let my beans cook dry then put 'em off." "The baby's got a stomach ache and I'm goin' to whip him." "The baby died. She had the yellow janders."

A little boy approaches. "Pack me my dinner, I've got to go to work, I swear I do!" A number of children seem to gravitate into this playhouse and automatically assume either the masculine or feminine roles without argument as to who is mother or daddy. This does not mean that there may not be exclusion of certain children, however: "Miss Lewis, we don't want her to live here." Nor does it mean that Marvin has taken on an effeminate role when he sits and rocks the baby doll, for this is just the way he sometimes sees his father rock his own baby brother.

Now Ina Lee is bathing a rubber doll and squirting water out of it. "She peeing!" she calls, and asks me to come and see. The children are interested, but do not seem to think this is anything "naughty" or anything to get silly over. It's like the time they saw me pouring grapefruit juice out of a can and exclaimed somewhat matter-of-factly that it, too, was "peeing." This word apparently can be used somewhat like the "cuss" words many of the children hurl out almost without thinking, as a natural part of their vocabulary, especially when they are angry.

That there are no inhibitions whatever about this kind of talk certainly is not the case, however. Even the use of this word, "pee," can sometimes be accompanied by a slight tinge of excitement, and remembered whippings may interfere somewhat—not very much —with a child's use of cuss words in the completely uninhibited fashion of some of the adults: "Why, my mother and daddy cuss all the time whenever they get mad." In fact, most of the children did not feel free to let down the barriers and cuss at all until about three months had passed.

But there are some words which all the children definitely feel to be decidedly naughty and forbidden. Such a word is "duty" when used to refer to a body excretion. When I first read the story in which Doody, the Rooster, is a character, the name brought on a chorus of rather embarrassed, excited giggles, which subsided as soon as I explained that the word was Doody and not Duty.

It very seldom happened, however, that the children used such words among themselves to giggle over, as had been the very common tendency in my group at the Harriet Johnson Nursery School, where the excitement would have become somewhat hysterical if not checked.

Buddy, the same little boy who had the excited laugh, went through a brief stage of bringing out these words at the lunch table, as the intellectual little Joey in the four's at the Harriet Johnson Nursery School did. "Eat chicken duty," Buddy would say, giggle, giggle. But often he failed to get any response from any of the other children, and after a few weeks he had forgotten all about it. Only once did I record that he worked himself up to a pitch that might in any way be called uncontrolled and hilarious. This was a year and a half after he had been in school.

The one occasion which elicited excited, uncontrolled, "bathroom" behavior on the part of Martin is interesting enough to go into in some detail. The whole situation clearly illustrates what it is that can call out this kind of response.

Martin was five and a half and had been in school for six months. We were all sitting in a circle, singing ballads. I sang the song about "Yon Yonson" to the children for the first time. For some reason this song sent Martin off into peals of giggles which he could not seem to control. Like Buddy (and like his own father!) whenever he laughed over anything it was in a way that seemed to be an uncontrolled letting-go of something pent up. "Yon Yonson" had the effect of intensifying this outbursting quality. While I was struggling to get this laughter quieted so that we could go on with the song, George suddenly gave Martin a great kick. The two boys started a fight there in the middle of the circle. I separated them and again began to cope with Martin's laughter which started right up again.

"Martin, the joke's over. We all want to sing some more. If you can't stop, suppose you go out on the porch and play there for a while."

He got up and started to dash in the opposite direction. I caught him and quickly carried him out to the porch—no doubt unwisely, since this must have been quite an ignominious experience for him to have to endure in the presence of his peers.

In a few moments he came back and sat down in his chair, red, excited, worked up. Instead of laughing he began to make mouthy noises and at the same time to point suggestively to his behind, trying to catch George's eye. He had been disgraced and had to retaliate in the worst way he knew to make up for a series of rather unbearable situations—first, the struggle against the giggle, which may have been really out of his control, then the furious kick from George, for which he had not had the opportunity to retaliate, and worst of all, his humiliating exit from the room.

This was an isolated instance. Such occurrences, on the part of Martin or any of the other children, were indeed very rare.

Nor did the children ever use any "shady" words as names for the adults in the school. "Miss Stink" or even "Dopey" uttered by a Cumberland mountain child would be almost as unthinkable as hostile, angry talk of killing the teacher and chopping down the school. Though certainly the five-year-old boys, and one who was six, occasionally relished talking in a somewhat bravado way, always in good humor though, and in fun. "I'll bust your nose if you don't, Miss Lewis!" or "Oh, you hush, Miss Lewis!" Such talk was not in evidence until at least a year had passed, however, and none of the children younger than five ever spoke in that way.

I think the truth of the matter may have been that these children never really felt that they wanted to chop down the school or send me, the representative of adult authority, sailing out of the window. It seemed that the need to rebel, the urge to resist adult control, so characteristic of the children in the Harriet Johnson Nursery School, was not one of J.W.'s driving impulses. And temper tantrums such as David's, or instances of actually fighting and hitting the teacher, or even of using verbal "aggression" against her were practically nonexistent during the whole two and a half years.

Of course there is also the possibility, which is an important one to keep in mind as we watch the children, that they may not have felt free to express the "worst" of such urges, even if they did have them. They may have dreaded the disapproval and punishment which they thought would follow, or their home training may have given them a strong sense of taboo about doing such "terrible" things as strike a teacher or call her dirty names.

Whatever may account for this placidity of the mountain children, this easy compliance to adult dictates, this relative lack of aggressive expression, it would seem that right here we may have come to the very heart of the distinction between David and J.W. We must stop and look more closely and carefully into this matter of aggression.

I do not mean to give the impression that the children were afraid to rebel in any way, or were afraid to correct me if I had misunderstood their intentions and mistakenly said "Don't." There was the time when I found our little three-year-old Marvin leaving the school with our broken hammer stowed away in his pocket. Very patiently I explained to him that I was sorry, he must leave the hammer at school, we had very few hammers and couldn't spare even this broken one, which we might find a way to fix some day. Marvin at that time was one of our shy, inarticulate children who never talked. He made no response—simply let me take the hammer from him and leave it in the school (as I thought). But he had his own idea and knew it was a good one, and was not to be deterred by my mistaken notions. He smuggled the hammer away after all, and to my great amazement his mother had it in her hand when she came out with Marvin to the nursery school car the next morning. It had a fine new handle in place of the old broken one. "Miss Lewis, here's your hammer. Marvin asked his dad to make a new handle for you."

And there were one or two occasions when a number of the children showed plenty of defiance, for good reason. I noticed that if I ever lost my patience and spoke to them in a cross, "bossy" manner—and unfortunately I did a few times—they bristled up immediately and stood their ground, refusing to do what I asked, behaving, in fact, just like their spirited, stubborn elders. But when I remained gentle and reasonable, so did they—an indication that the teacher's part in the picture can be a considerable one and is not to be neglected in the attempt to understand the behavior of the children. Watch Wayne Edward in the swing. He cannot resist the temptation to keep on swinging, though play time is up and he should be helping to carry in the toys and boxes and boards. I am finding it difficult, in the heat, to carry so much heavy material with no other adult assistance and at the same time keep my eye on the children and wind up the day at the right time. I lose my patience after several unsuccessful gentle attempts to dislodge the boy from the swing. "Wayne Edward, did I say to swing or did I say to put away your toys?" I finally call out in exasperation. Does Wayne Edward thereupon leap out of the swing and run to do his work? No indeed. He stays right where he is, defiantly, for a few more moments, making an impudent little grimace to boot.

And again on another day, when I have impatiently accosted him and Virginia and Ina Lee as they dawdle over putting away some blocks they have knocked down, defiance is the first response I get. They only kick at the blocks and make no move to put them away. Because of situations such as these, one wonders if the children might have had on "company manners" for me much of the time, lapsing into their home behavior when I became more like the adults to whom they were accustomed at home! Or do these instances simply demonstrate that the children *could* rebel when good occasion arose, and it was therefore not entirely a matter of fear that the occasion or need seldom arose? (Note, however, that "rebel" here means disobey, but not strike, spit, or throw a tantrum.)

Of course, there were children who seemed to have more urge for independence than others. There were some who went through mischievous or defiant phases, one or two who "tried me out" during their first days in school to see how much they could get away with, others who would now and then make a little show of rebellion at putting away playthings, or settling down to rest. There was Marvin who could screw his face up into a sassy little pout when it was necessary for me to speak to him several times about keeping his muddy shoes off the seat of the car (few of the children lived near enough to walk to school), even though this pout would dissolve into a self-conscious grin as soon as he saw me looking at him. There was J.B. who "talked back" impudently to cover up his embarrassment after he had just spilled a plateful of graham crackers. Indeed, there were many instances of the transitory sort of rebellion one expects of small children. The point is that on the whole such rebellion was transitory, infrequent, mild in character, and no real problem to a teacher. During the entire time there were only two children (out of about forty) whose consistent urge to rebel marked them off from the others—rough, stormy George, who had been ill a good deal as a baby, and according to his mother was "awfully spoiled" as a result, and mild, twinkling-eyed little Virginia, who had her own ideas from the very first day and stuck by them, playfully but firmly.

As for the others—watch them. A few of them now have asked me if they may climb the fence and go over into the beautiful pine grove adjoining us to pick up pine cones. This is not our property, and we are not supposed to play there, but I tell the children I am sure that it will be quite all right for them to go over just to pick up pine cones, but not to stay long, not to go far. They climb over the fence and I, if I want to, can turn my back on them and forget them. There is no question about it—they will not run off, they will not go far, they will soon be back.

And what reasonableness they show on the day when I have to

"This little Summerville nursery school"

"These mountain children went through exactly the same stages of design painting observable in the Harriet Johnson Nursery School"

"On seeing them for the first time out playing in their yards, leaving for school or nursery school, or walking down the roads, one would find it difficult to lump them together as all of a kind"

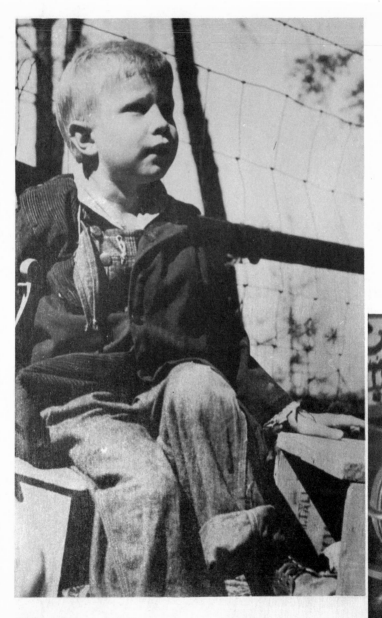

"They appear to be normally developed,
healthy, attractive children"

is obvious that they
people who have an up-
ht, if not stern, tradition
ind them"

"Scarcely any of his parents' activities go on without
his little face somewhere in the picture"

"The little boys take after their fathers"

"As accepted as the love his family gives him, as the dangerous hot stove in the middle of the room, as the place that is his as a member of a community even though he is just a baby"

"These tin can playhouses, as integral to the scene as the big black washing pot behind the house, or the swing on the porch"

"Summerville children of ten seem to be, in some ways, small adults"

"Hauling home the stovewood"

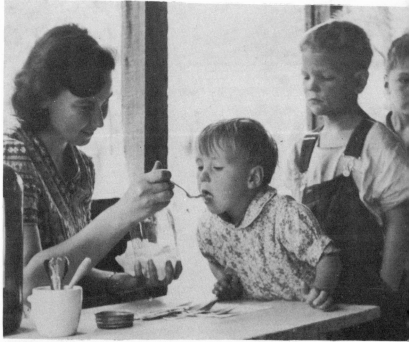

"This placidity of the mountain children, this easy
compliance to adult dictates"

"A strange visitor is someone to peek at shyly
from around the corner of the house"

"There were one or two occasions when a number
of the children showed plenty of defiance"

"His sisters and even his brothers will grab him up and cuddle him, for these boys never heard it suggested that it might be sissy for them to fondle and care for babies"

"With a five-year-old protector affectionately guarding her"

"And this outdoor life helps to give him
a certain sturdiness"

nowing very little of a home that provides
at is not absolutely necessary"

"At peace with their world"

"He is king in his cabin"

drive into town for graham crackers, after I have picked up only five of the children. They go into the grocery store with me and are presented with enormous lollypops by the grocery man. This is not an everyday occurrence for them by any means, and they tear into the lollypops with the greatest delight. As we start on our way again, teacher ponders what to do, concerned that none of the other children will have lollypops, and that so much sweetness is being consumed before the more nourishing mid-morning lunch. Finally I stop the car and explain to them that I think it is too bad that the other children will just have to sit and watch them sucking lollypops. How about giving them to me to keep, all separately wrapped and named, until it is time to go home? Every lollypop is handed over without a whimper.

Is it true that there never was a trace of a temper tantrum among these children? If a temper tantrum means flopping down on the floor and kicking and screaming in uncontrolled rage, yes, it is true. "Sulking" was one of the typical reactions of the children when frustrated. Look at Junior. I have explained as sympathetically as I know how to that he will simply have to let Richard have one of his trucks for a while. He goes off pouting, sits alone on a bench for twenty minutes, refusing to play with anything at all until it is again his turn to have the truck he wants. Even the two children who might have been considered my Davids did not resort to actual tantrums when thwarted. They would light out and hit at *things*. I can still hear George cussing, on one of his bad days, and see him violently smashing away with his hammer at that chicken coop he was trying to take apart.

The only real tantrum that occurred during the school day was on the part of a little city child who was visiting us for a few weeks. One morning, in a frenzy of rage at being taken away from his mother, he hurled his bottle of milk out of the open window of the car onto the road. The effect of this on my mountain children was as if some apparition from another world, some unheard-of outlander, had suddenly descended in our midst. They sat there awed, open-mouthed.

And did these children really never once attempt to hit the

teacher or student teachers? Yes, there were a few times, perhaps three or four, when the children who did it seemed to be involved in intense emotional situations that were more than they could handle. (The question comes to mind immediately, do the Harriet Johnson children become emotionally involved and deeply distressed much more frequently and easily?) Wayne Edward had been out of school for three weeks. He was consumed with shyness when it was time to return, and held back. But I finally managed to persuade him to get into the car, and the ride to school was pleasant enough. When we arrived at the schoolhouse, however, he was again overwhelmed with self-consciousness, and bit at my wrist as I took him by the hand to lead him along.

And little three-year-old J.B., who was probably the most timid child who ever came to the school, had also bitten and scratched at me for the same reason, during the very first month of school. His dad had come along to visit for a minute, on his way home. When he left, J.B. wanted to follow, and was beside himself with despair when I held him back.

And were these children incapable of tough, rough talk? No indeed! The older ones, especially, were masters of it, but seemed to have no need—or willingness?—to use it against adults in the nursery school. Occasionally there was "ganging up" against one of the other children. Little "Mac," for some reason, was one they picked on. "Do you like Mac?" one boy would say to another. "No! I could beat the guts plum out o' him!"

And the barrage of violence they could sometimes loose against what seemed to them a quite legitimate object fairly took away my breath the first time I heard it, toward the end of our two years. A strange car was parked near one of the children's homes as we drove up. Edward recognized it as the sheriff's car. "It's the jail men!" Whereupon Buddy threatened, "They'd better not come to my house where my daddy is. I'll knock the dukee (duty) out of them . . . I'll get my daddy's shot gun." There was a good deal of genuine and deep-seated emotion in this, because the boy's father had spent a year in prison.

But the climax came on the day we picked up a little neighbor boy who began telling us, with solemn eyes, about the "mean" aunt who had lived with them once. "Was she *mean*! She'd cuss . . . and she was mean to God!" Whereupon Wayne Edward, who also knew this aunt, chimed in that "She sure was mean. I wish your dad would cut her throat and knock her in the jaw so her teeth fall out."

Yes, in such situations this kind of verbal aggression must have seemed to the children entirely permissible, if not laudable, and it was easily indulged in.

Indeed, as we have seen, the Summerville children indulged to some extent in a number of forms of aggression: they sometimes fought with each other, they struck out angrily at *things,* they cussed and occasionally used other "dirty" talk. One wonders again if the one expression of aggression which was conspicuously lacking—that directed toward adults in the nursery school—was absent because there actually existed small urge for it or because the children did not dare to show it, or whether both of these factors were operating at the same time.

But we have been examining only one aspect of the picture of aggression. We have scarcely looked at what is usually considered its inevitable concomitant—fearfulness—even to see if there are any traces of it. A consideration of this angle may help to clarify our picture.

We might reasonably expect to find that children who are only mildly aggressive are at the same time not greatly troubled with fears of any sort. It is the distressed, uprooted child, the one who has lost his sense of anchorage and comfort and safety, who is apt to resort to excessive aggressiveness in the attempt to restore his equilibrium,—unless powerful repressions are at work to restrain him from showing such feelings.

I have mentioned that some of the younger children in the Summerville Nursery School sucked their thumbs. Should we assume, according to the common theory, that this is a sign of "insecurity"? And was the thumb-sucking in Summerville comparable to the amount and kind observed in the Harriet Johnson Nursery School?

There were only four or five children in the mountain nursery school who ever seemed to resort to it, and they were all the younger ones, most of them three years old, one four. I believe I never saw a thumb in the mouth of an older child.

I first noticed it at a time when the group of children was very assorted as to ages. Our youngest was two and a half, our oldest over six. As I have mentioned before, the littler ones, in the presence of many bigger, older children, seemed somewhat overshadowed and overawed. It was chiefly during that first hour in the morning that thumbs went into mouths, as the little ones sat around trying to decide what to play. When the older ones "graduated" or went off by themselves with the student teacher, the thumb-sucking thinned out at once. And at no time did even the littlest ones suck their thumbs when they were settling down to rest after lunch—though this statement should be qualified somewhat with the explanation that we had a rest period at school and an afternoon program for only four months out of the two and a half years, and that one of the thumb-suckers was not present during these four months.

It is difficult to make an exact, quantitative sort of comparison between the two groups in this matter of thumb-sucking, since I never attempted to follow the children around with a stop watch. However, there may be some meaning in the general observation that five out of twelve mountain children were seen to suck their thumbs during a morning in Tennessee, compared with ten out of thirteen four-year-olds at the Harriet Johnson Nursery School, and that I detected thumbs going into mouths at eight different times during that day in Tennessee compared with twenty-eight times in New York. Also, it was noticeable that four or five of the Harriet Johnson children clung to their thumbs or fingers most of the morning, as best they could while playing a good deal at the same time, whereas thumb-sucking among the mountain children was a more sporadic sort of thing, occurring only now and then during inactive moments in the morning and chiefly at the very beginning of the day before play was well launched. If thumb-sucking is a refuge for children, if it does indicate that all is not going well, we must conclude that the troubling situations giving rise to a need to resort to it do not exist for the Summerville children to the same extent that they do for the Harriet Johnson children, provided, of course, that both groups feel equally free to indulge in it.

Are there any other traits among the children that might seem to point to the existence of some "fearfulness"? On the surface, it might appear that the extreme shyness of the children is an expression of fear or insecurity. But as we shall see as we go along, this kind of shyness is typical not only of the children but of the majority of the adults in Summerville. Let us consider, for the time being, that restraint in the presence of the outlander is but the accepted mode of behavior for young and old alike in this community.

Are there children who are afraid to "hit back"? Who run cringing and crying to teacher when any child starts to attack? On the whole, such behavior is conspicuously lacking. We can, however, point to Ernestine, who has been an outstandingly fearful child from the beginning. Here she comes now, running to me and almost screaming, because the boys are chasing her with the "locusts" that have descended upon us in such hoards. These boys have always been able to torment Ernestine very easily, so are tempted to make the most of their opportunity.

And when we ride home at noon, Ernestine will begin tearfully begging me over and over, even before we leave the school building, not to drive off from her house till she finds out for sure that her mother is there. When we actually drive up and park by her fence, she walks along hesitantly, calling out, "Mother! Mother!" at the same time looking back anxiously at me in the car, though never once have I failed to wait for her. If she finds that the gate is locked, she comes running back to the car in a panic of tears. Or if the noon train should come along while we are parked there, she will start to cry and wait to get out of the car until the train has passed.

As I have said, such a picture of fearfulness is unusual, and is fairly easily understood in the light of her home background, which differs in some important respects from that of most of the other children, as we shall see later.

There are others who have some fears of animals, for instance. Little new Barbara, two and a half, was terrified over the friendly, barking dogs at the Folk School, and likewise over the roaring motorcycle belonging to the boy next door to the school.

And I am inclined to think that the play of crashing up the toy cars and trucks and getting them "mired up," which was so never-endingly popular among many of the children, may have indicated a real fear of such situations, possibly engendered by our daily ride. To be sure, there were a few occasions during the worst of the winter weather when we did get mired up in the muddy ruts out in the "Cove," trying to turn the car around. At such times I was always aware of pairs of anxious eyes fixed profoundly on mine, to read the verdict. I felt that if I had ever shown a trace of fear or distress myself, the anxiety in those eyes might have turned to panic. (Needless to say, I always leaped out of the car with all the joviality and unconcern I could muster, assuring the children that it was nothing, that we would be out in a minute—and fortune was always with us!)

"Anxiety," too, might describe the way in which some of the children, especially those who were new in the school, kept watching my face all during the day to see if they were doing the right things. Edward was washing his hands before lunch. He took the small white, smooth cake of Ivory soap and rubbed it gently on his face, obviously enjoying the feel of it. But suddenly he noticed that I was watching him. Not realizing that I was merely vicariously sharing his pleasure in the soap, he hastily brought his hands down and proceeded to wash them, in a very business-like way, with guilt (as well as soap) spread all over his face. In the same way, the fights of some of the new children evaporated into thin air, as I have already mentioned, when I merely looked toward those who were fighting. Here is evidence that some of these children did not feel entirely free to be themselves, as I have suggested may have been the case. The presence of this kind of anxiety—fear of doing the thing that teacher might not approve of—may very well indicate that the placidity and obedience and peacefulness of the children was not entirely a matter of their spontaneously feeling obedient. Though it must be kept in mind that a gradual process of "loosening up" in my presence did take place during the course of the two years. Edward might not have hesitated to play with the soap if he had not been so new in the school. As we have seen, the boys who had been with me from the start gradually lost their inhibitions about cussing and acting silly, and even became free enough to talk to me in a bravado way, if not to whack me heartily on the back by way of pleasant greeting, while passing. One could scarcely say that they did not "feel free to be themselves," unless there was just one length to which they could not allow themselves to go—pugnacious resistance to their teacher.

One day I asked the children to tell me what they were afraid of. Trains, trucks, and cars were the most common answers, though some mentioned such unrealities as tigers, bobcats, and "the Boogerman"—and even "that old Willkie!" (This was at election time.) Two children in the same family could think of nothing at all that frightened them, or perhaps I should say were not able to tell me of anything.

It seemed to me that the fears and anxieties of these children were largely the product of their living conditions or home training. Except in the case of Ernestine, I did not feel that they were tinged with deep emotional disturbances that might differentiate them from the fears to be expected as a part of their cultural pattern.

However, it is important to keep in mind the fact that the fears observed by me, an "outlander," may not have been the only ones that actually existed. Fears are much more easily detected in children who express themselves readily and throw themselves into their play with an imagination that completely transfigures them (as the Harriet Johnson children did) than in the case of those to whom the flow of words does not come with the power and ease of a waterfall, who are not accustomed to practically losing their identities when they play, and indeed hold themselves off in a shy restraint for weeks, if not months, at a time. Of course, one can also ask, when children's play lacks imaginative intensity, is there not the possibility that this may indicate the absence of fears and conflicts that otherwise would probably become evident in some degree? We must remember that the Summerville children showed no hesitance in playing out their fear of car accidents.

But all this while we have been considering the David qualities, neglecting the Stephen characteristics which are no less important and no less indicative of the differences between these two groups of children. I have said only that most of the children gradually developed more of these Stephen qualities than they seemed to possess in the beginning.

They came to love stories almost more than anything else. Especially on a very cold morning it was common to see a number of the children run for the picture books as soon as they arrived, pull up the chairs and benches around the stove, and sit there for a good half hour, contentedly warming themselves and looking at the books—and begging for story after story.

Painting and crayoning also became favorite occupations, especially among the girls, so favorite, in fact, that to keep a supply of paper on hand sufficient to satisfy their avid interest was quite a problem to me. But in spite of this interest, the designs the children painted (their pictures were almost never representations of any actual object), could not have been called astonishingly beautiful. An interesting thing it was, too, because these mountain children went through exactly the same stages of design painting observable in the Harriet Johnson Nursery School. Mere dabs gradually expanded into shapes that bore relation to each other, stripes appeared, dots appeared, then whole sheets solidly covered with color. But whatever it was in Stephen that enabled him to produce designs and color combinations of really flashing beauty simply was not a part of J.W.'s make-up; or, if such possibilities did lie dormant within him, they failed to flower during the time I knew him.

Likewise block building never appealed greatly to J.W. as a way of creating beautiful balanced form. Most of his buildings were very utilitarian structures, with little that was decorative about them. Not that he was incapable of creating an architectural unit of real beauty—Buddy, in fact, went through a brief phase of experimenting in several kinds of very artistic forms—but on the whole he did not care to, and I could not spur him on to this kind of activity "for teeth or toenails," as Ina Lee's old grandmother would say.

Nor did J.W. and Johnnie May enter into rhythms at any time with quite the spirited joy, energy, and inventiveness of the Harriet Johnson children. This comparison may be a somewhat unfair one because of the circumstances under which we tried to have rhythms at our little Summerville school. We had only a very small room and no piano. Accompaniment had to be either my feeble singing, or drum beating and clapping. For only a month— the last month I was there—were we able to use the large room at the Highlander Folk School where there was a piano.

While I expected the children to be self-conscious when we first went over to this big room (and many of them were), I thought surely they would gradually learn to enter in with freedom and fun. However, I found that it was an up-hill struggle to keep them interested. I tried every variety of rhythms I had ever heard about, and some that I had never heard about, but still every day there were stragglers over to the bench, which was the place for sitting and watching. Was I using too much of their energy in these rhythmic exercises? I cut out all the energetic things and concentrated on very quiet little musical games. In the end I had found a few things that appealed to all of the children—very simple little patterned dramatizations of trains, cars, and other things with which they were familiar—and many games that appealed to only a few. The bench was filled a good part of the time with children who were either too tired, too uninterested, or too self-conscious to join in. Little Edward, who had been coming to school for a year and a half, could never bring himself to do more than just walk around with the others. As soon as any dancelike motions of feet or hands were required, he dropped out.

A longer experiment might have produced somewhat different results; and indeed our long "experiment" or practice in imaginative thinking and the creative use of language did in the end reveal in many of the children sparks quite worthy of Stephen.

That this, too, was something of an up-hill climb, however, was certainly the case. For instance, Stephen and his playmates needed very little encouragement to arrive at the conclusion that a thermometer rising was one of the "quietest things in the world." But when I first sat down with the Summerville children and suggested that just for fun (though from my point of view it was for purposes of sharpening imaginative thinking), we try to name all the "fast" things we could think of, the answers were of the most obvious sort—"trucks, dogs, horses." And some of the children needed a good deal of prodding to get away from the idea that because these had been the correct answers for the "fast" discussion, they were not also the correct answers when we sat down together and tried to think of all the things that were very "quiet."

But listen to them now, after two years of "practice." "My hands is cold as a copperhead," says Ella Caroline. I ask if the children can think of some other cold things. "Cold as concrete!" "Cold as 'taters!" "Cold as iron!" "Cold as sheets at night!"

And we stop the car one day to watch the dismantling of the old ruined cabin little Frank had lived in. Not much more than the chimney stands now. It is strange to think that just last week Frank was living there. We are a little sad as we watch. Then Marvin, remembering his favorite story, sums up our sentiments almost as Stephen would have done. Says he, philosophically, "What's gone is gone."

Are there real differences, then, between J.W. and Stephen and David?

Some of the differences may appear to be a matter of degree. The mountain children probably have less physical energy than the Harriet Johnson children—a fact which may to a large measure explain their comparative inactivity, comparative peacefulness. Likewise, IQ scores of the two groups would seem to indicate, on the surface at least, that there is a considerably lower level of intelligence among the mountain children—though this is dangerous ground to tread on. We have no way of knowing what would happen to the IQ of a mountain child who grew up in the stimulating environment pressing upon the New York child at every turn.

We have seen that Cumberland mountain children can develop some of the same kind of creative originality that distinguishes the Harriet Johnson children so markedly. Even Cumberland mountain children, so shy in the beginning, can become very noisy, can giggle now and then over "dirty" words, can boast toughly of their powers to kill and shoot, can sometimes fight and hit each other for what they want, can gang up against certain of their peers, can rebel on occasion.

And here we come to the outstanding difference between the two groups. "Rebel on occasion," I say. But why does the occasion arise so seldom among the mountain children, and why, when it does arise, are the manifestations of rebellion so mild in character? Why doesn't J.W. ever hit the teacher and call her Dope, and fling himself on the floor in a tantrum? Likewise, why are his conflicts with the other children, and indeed all of his aggressive expressions colored with less emotional intensity than David's? And why, whether or not it has any connection with his aggressiveness, is his creative output also lacking in what we might call the "intensity" that characterizes Stephen's?

Here we see that we cannot meaningfully describe such differences as a matter of "degree." The factors responsible for them are imbedded in the particular kind of home and community conditions, standards, patterns, under which the children grow up.

What manner of place is this Summerville, Tennessee? Are its children strictly disciplined into behaving—through threats, punishments, or through the influence of a stern social code of right and wrong? Are they afraid to rebel?

Or should we think of the Summerville children as having

little need to rebel as they live along comfortably secure in their status in their families, happy and safe in the warmth of their homes, at peace with their limited world?

Is it the small world they live in or the code under which they are brought up that largely accounts for the comparatively mediocre quality of their creative accomplishments?

Or is there no one answer to any of these questions?

INTRODUCTION TO SUMMERVILLE

❀❀❀❀❀❀❀❀❀❀❀❀❀❀❀❀❀❀❀❀❀❀❀❀

SUMMERVILLE, TENNESSEE. Perhaps the best way to orient the reader toward this community is to emphasize at the outset that the region in which it is located, on the Cumberland Plateau fifty miles from Chattanooga, cannot be considered typical of the really isolated Southern mountain sections occasionally described by writers who are captivated by the old timers and the old ways. In fact, to a true mountaineer, say from the depths of the Kentucky mountains, one whose children scarcely know what ice cream is, Summerville would seem to be civilization itself. That many elements of an isolated mountain culture persist here is true. There are still mountain wives who scarcely stir out of their homes and are too shy to talk to callers; grandmothers who still speak an Elizabethan language; young folks who carry on their courtin' by means of secret trysts and notes left under the stone by the gate. But they live next door to modern young high school girls who try out the latest hairdo's, go dancing at night in the honky-tonks on the highway, and hum the popular songs of our time. Summerville is still in many ways an "old-time" community, but it is one that is in the process of emerging from isolation into participation in modern life.

Another way to characterize the Summerville that Johnnie May and J.W. know is to say that it represents one of the realities behind a group of rather startling county statistics: "60% of the total population on relief . . . the net resources of 94.2% of the relief families average less than $500 . . . total indebtedness of relief families, in per cent of all property, over 50%." *

This is a land that can no longer support its population. The

* Figures from *Public Welfare and Related Problems in Grundy Co., Tennessee* (American Public Welfare Association, Chicago, 1940).

sandy, unproductive soil of this plateau never was fit for farming. Back in the 1840s before the discovery of coal, there were only a dozen or so families scattered between the neighborhood of Summerville and the foot of the mountain—pioneers trying to make a living off the land. Then came coal and the railroad and work in the timber. People flocked to the mountain. In the 1870s the mines were booming.

Now, some seventy years later, only one large mine continues to function. The coal veins are worked out. And 213,000 acres of cut-over land in a second growth of scrub oaks are all that is left of the timber.

As a result, the ex-miners, ex-lumbermen who are J.W.'s parents have had nothing to turn to but relief, and road repair under the W.P.A. for a wage that has varied from $19.20 to $32.40 a month. In the evening they come home to weathered two- or three-room houses that are little better than shacks. Even most of those left from the boom days no longer show any traces of paint.

These Summerville homes have no electricity, no plumbing. Some even have no outhouses, no screens. Inside there is scarcely room to move about because of the beds—beds for six or eight or ten children, and for grandmother, or for married daughter and husband who all live under the same roof.

But perhaps Summerville can best be understood by visualizing the community in terms of the various kinds of roads that lead to it and become a part of it. That there are these various roads is in itself a significant key not only to the community's geographical situation but to its sociological position as well.

One might think of the U.S. highways with their fast-moving interstate traffic as symbolic of our modern technological civilization. One of these highways—main artery between Chattanooga and Nashville, and also between Chicago and Florida—swings up our mountain and down on the other side, leaving on the top of the plateau a collection of gas stations, modern tourist cabins, and roadside cafes with their juke boxes, that goes by the name of Piedmont, Tennessee. Summerville is back in the woods behind the highway, only two miles away, but certainly the Florida-bound, even if they could see past the wall of gas stations lining the highway, would never guess its existence.

That Summerville is entirely untouched by the life that this highway for the most part has created is, of course, not the case. Summerville's men walk to Piedmont for groceries, and a few of the young boys and girls find employment in the cafes and gas stations—employment by day and entertainment by night, at least in the honky-tonks. Some of the women, too, find summer work, cleaning, cooking, washing, on the grounds of the big resort where solid Southern families have been spending their summers for the past fifty years—though this resort was accessible by railway long before the highway was built and has always been something apart from the highway town.

As a matter of fact, the highway was not completed until 1924. Before that time the main road up the mountain was a rough and rocky one-way toll road. Bringing the highway in was like laying a paved strip of modern civilization through what was largely a horse-and-buggy realm.

A paved state highway—paved within the last fifteen years—turns off at Piedmont, cuts through Summerville, and leads north to the county seat and the coal mining town. But few of Summerville's homes are built along this highway, and its traffic, though slower and less cosmopolitan than that of the interstate highway, bears little relation to the life of a small community like Summerville. This state highway belongs to the mail bus, to the coal trucks that rumble along to and from the small one-man mines, and especially it belongs to the small towns of the county—Dyersville, Selby, Montvale. It is a part of their life.

Look at Dyersville, four miles north of Summerville. This is a sprawling town of about 2,000 inhabitants. A ruined stone roundhouse by the station and a brick company-store with an iron railing torn and drooping from what was once meant to look like a balcony are evidence that the town once saw better days. Here, too, are the other landmarks of the small town in the midst of a rural area: the county high school building, the old brick courthouse with its upper and lower porches and its jail in one wing, the white wooden churches, Methodist, Baptist, Episcopal, the bank, the lumber yard, a few old Victorian mansions that were once homes of the coal and railroad magnates, and the movie, in front of which you would probably stand for some time in bewilderment, trying to figure out which placard advertized the show of the day. The parts of this scattered little town where the wooden false-front stores line the street suggest somewhat the scene of a Wild West movie.

But this town and the others as seen from the state highway give very little idea of the nature and extent of the county's population. To find the people of the rural communities, you must always leave the highway. Follow the little dirt roads to the right and left, all along the way.

Now that we have left the highways behind and have come to these unpaved roads where there is little traffic, we can begin to talk about Summerville. Now we are back in the kerosene lamp and muddy road era, before the days of widespread use of automobiles, radios, movies, telephones, and daily newspapers. But this is as far back as we can go. Here in Summerville we will not find roads that are no more than rocky creek beds over which the traveler must make his slow way on horseback, roads leading to an even older era in which clothes, for instance, are all woven and made at home, "free school" is held one month out of the year by a man who can count a dozen eggs, and almost nothing is ever purchased from a store. No, the highways have come in, bringing the mail buses and the Sears Roebuck catalogs. The mail car gets around very well even on Summerville's unpaved dirt roads.

These reddish roads wind through the woods and clearings, and Summerville's sixty houses trail along beside them. Here on one road (called "Branchtown," though there is no signpost), a number are grouped fairly closely together. Others have no neighbors nearer than a half mile away. In places, what was once the old stagecoach road fades out entirely, leaving a house or two perched along the way, indicating where it used to run.

There are no stores in Summerville, with the exception of one small general store on the highway, too far on the outskirts for much patronage from our community. And there are no signs of industry except for the railroad track running parallel to the highway. If you arrive early enough, you will see the morning train of the day making its trip down the mountain from the coal mine twenty miles away.

The two-room elementary school out by the highway, three small wooden churches (Seventh Day Adventist, Methodist, and Church of Christ), and a comfortable-looking brown house with a sign over the gate, "Highlander Folk School," are the only striking evidences of community life, aside from the homes themselves.

I have described these houses as "shacks." That they are all alike is of course not the case. Here and there on our corner of the plateau are a few old cabins of hand-hewn logs—the typical "picturesque" mountain cabin. Then there are the houses of the boom days that must have been somewhat pretentious when they were new, three- and four-room houses with two stories and gingerbread decorations on the porches. Lastly, there are the cabins of the familiar "box" type, successor to the log cabin all through the Southern mountains. These are the houses that have been built for the sons and daughters of the ex-miners as they marry. They are two- or three-room cabins of rough lumber, hastily erected, seldom painted.

Though there are of course some exceptions—a few homes with electric lights, radios, pianos, well-kept flower gardens—the general impression of these Summerville houses is one of small, bare "shacks" that have gone to seed on barren land.

The trouble with many of them (barring lack of space, conveniences, paint, repairs), is that they seem unattached to the land. Perched up there on their foundation stones or wooden posts, with no greenery to hide the dark spaces beneath them, they have an old, toothless look. And even in the yards where there are grassy places and lilac bushes, much of the ground may be tramped bare by children, dogs, and chickens, and often is left littered with old shoes, tin cans, chamber pots, and discarded kitchen utensils. True, most families clean up their yards in the spring, and in the summer the abundant green of the foliage and fields gives the locality a certain beauty. But in the winter the trees, the houses, and the land all settle into a barren, unrelieved five months' gray.

But stop now, and look more closely at one of these Summerville homes. I choose this one because it is representative of Branchtown Road, and of the kind of home that the majority of the nursery school children have come from. It stands there bare, in the midst of its six acres of cleared land. The tall weedy grass and the five old apple trees by the side of the house are not sufficient to tie it to the land. There are no vines, no bushes. Or is it the lack of paint and the droop of the front porch that give this house its appearance of having been cast up adrift? The porch slopes so much toward the step that the back legs of the chairs have been sawed off a little, to make the chairs comfortable for sitting.

This house, though fairly small and only one story high, was one of those "fine" ones built in the prosperous days. Undoubtedly it once had a coat of paint.

The roof on the back wing must be the original one. Its shingles (or "boards") now have a ruffled appearance. The front wing has been covered fairly recently with tin roofing. But the house is far from rain- or windproof. Most of the window panes are just squares cut from old cardboard cartons. All told, there must be at least twenty "window lights" out.

The open door gives a glimpse of a small dark room which seems to be filled with beds and very little else—a lamp on the dresser, a calendar on the wall, a chair or two. There is no rug or covering of any kind on the rough, worn floor, and the heavy blue paper on the walls is rain-stained and peeling.

Out by the gate is the coal pile, crudely covered with sheets of tin. And what is this assemblage of old tin cans, boxes, little bits of broken crockery, empty gasoline cans over by the fence corner? No, not a dumping place, but the carefully arranged "playhouse" of the children who live here. All up and down Branch-town Road, everywhere in Summerville, in or near almost every yard where there are children, you see these tin-can playhouses, as integral to the scene as the big black washing pot behind the house or the swing on the porch.

The old outhouse over by the apple trees slants precariously —but at least there is an outhouse.

The barn here is across the road—just a small shed it is, about a third the size of the house. This family is lucky enough to own a cow and some chickens, but no horse (county statistics again: "56.0% of all relief farmers have no dairy cows"). Dogs go without saying—pups for the children and a couple of hounds for the man of the house who likes to go fox hunting.

The horse you see pulling the harrow out in the field beside the house belongs to one of the neighbors who rents his horse out in the spring, when everyone needs one for plowing. (Each family usually manages to grow a few such vegetables as potatoes, beans, corn and cabbage, to help out during the winter.) The man guiding the horse is not a man at all, but a little boy about nine. He must be learning how to do this work. His father stands there by the house watching him, and with him is another boy a few years older, who now runs out to take his turn.

This householder—he is our little Marvin's father—is a slight young man about thirty-five, but you who see him for the first time might easily judge him to be in his forties, misled by the lines in his rough face, by his drooping shoulders, and by the hair that sticks out stiffly from under his old cap like a doll's wig—to say nothing of the ragged overalls and bunchy jacket. Not that every man in Summerville looks just like this. There are individualities here as there are in any community. Certainly this man's "haircut" is more or less individual, in spite of the long-haired mountaineers in the funny papers. As a matter of fact, on Branchtown Road there are at least two men and one woman who "cut hair" for their children and their neighbors—one even goes to the near-by CCC Camp as professional barber—and a very good job they do of it.

But generally speaking, the Summerville men do have the weathered look this man has—the rough look of men who work outdoors. And that applies to their hats and overalls as well as to their faces and hands.

The wives who come to the doors and porches of these houses to look at us as we pass are not so easy to describe in a sentence. Out of a crude two-room shack comes a young mother—Ella Caroline's mother—all ready to go to a meeting of some kind, perhaps a P.T.A. meeting at the public school. She is erect, neatly combed, dressed with taste and style in a pretty silk-print dress. Her neighbor who comes out of the house across the road to join her even has a permanent wave (from the beauty shop in Piedmont) and red fingernails. But next door, standing on the porch, is a thin, hollow-chested, stooped woman, mother of many, face lined, teeth gone, oily hair pulled into a knot behind, an unbelievably dirty "garment" hung on her. She is in stocking feet, and is seldom seen at any kind of meeting or social gathering.

But the fact that she is mother of many does not necessarily account for her appearance. Around the bend a piece is another mother of many, of ten in fact. A large, buxom, energetic-looking woman she is, with a young face and a clean white apron. Understandably enough, some of the housewives have given in to the difficulties of living where water must be carried and all conveniences are lacking. Others have maintained high standards in a way that seems downright heroic.

This cursory glance at Summerville women shows apparently only dissimilarities, but we get an inkling of what they have in common by the cordial, natural way they all greet us, without barriers of sophistication. And if we should happen to see them in the privacy of their back yards on a wash day, even these dissimilarities would tend to slough off. Without the distractions of red fingernails, curled hair, and best dresses, the texture of their faces becomes more apparent. These women have the look of those who have known hard physical work all their lives.

We are already somewhat acquainted with the children. We know what they say and how they act, but perhaps have not a very clear idea of how they look. On seeing them for the first time out playing in their yards, leaving for school or nursery school, or walking down the roads, one would find it difficult to lump them together as all of a kind, or to say "Ha, these are mountain children!"

Here is a child whose legs and arms are covered with sores, and another whose eyes do not focus correctly. Here, again, are one or two, like Annie Pearl and Marvin, who look very frail and small; but for the most part they appear to be normally developed, healthy, attractive children, though some are nicely dressed and well cared for and others are far from clean and are literally in rags. Chronic colds and poor resistance to winter weather, characteristic of most of them, are not apparent to the casual observer.

The little boys take after their fathers. You see them everywhere, out in the fields following the plows, hauling home the stovewood, playing with the dogs in their yard—little blond, barefoot boys in somewhat ragged, somewhat dirty overalls. (But if it were a Sunday, and we happened to see the family starting out to Sunday School, those same little boys would have on their clean Sunday overalls, and their hair would be neatly slicked down with water.)

Like their mothers, the little girls are not so easy to characterize. These two, Ella Caroline and her sister, climbing into the nursery school car, are not only chubby and rosy but are immaculately clean and are dressed in dainty, starched, *white* clothing—a contrast to Emma Doris down the road whose scalp has been unwashed for so long that even other children begin to notice the dark places showing under the light hair, or to the Hunt sisters whose great brown bloomers emerge and hang below their crudely homemade dresses.

Bare feet, or white sandals; black bloomers coarsely stitched in white thread, or crisp little dresses; frowzled, unwashed hair, or permanent waves—there is almost no homogeneity in appearance. But just watch each one of these children hang her head and freeze up shyly when you, a stranger, greet her!

So this is Summerville. These are her people. When I first came here, an "outlander" from the North and the West, a number of things struck me as unusual, or at least unfamiliar. They became the landmarks that helped me get my bearings and "place" Summerville historically and economically and socially in relation to other communities in which I had lived. It seemed strange to me that people said "Howdy" instead of "Hello"; that hogs ran loose everywhere, even on the streets and sidewalks of the towns; that everyone you met on the road spoke to you, whether you knew him or not; that children had fancy double names like Ruby Jewel and Willie May; that twigs of the black-gum tree were used for "toothbrushes," that children were told to say "Yes ma'am" to me. And I was surprised that the mothers seemed to understand very well what the nursery school was all about even though they were people of very little "education." For the first time I heard "hit" for "it" and "thang" for "thing"; and also for the first time, though I visited in many small, bare shacks that were spotlessly clean and neat, I found myself in "homes" so cluttered with flies, trash, dirty clothes, so crowded with unclean beds, so littered and dark that I came away practically shaking, unable to grasp the fact that people lived in them.

A NEW BABY COMES TO SUMMERVILLE

✿✿✿✿✿✿✿✿✿✿✿✿✿✿✿✿✿✿✿✿✿✿

HERE IS A HOME where there will soon be a new baby. This is one of the more "picturesque" houses—from the outside. It looks less barren than the one described in the last chapter, because of the huge oak tree under which it is built and, though it also dates from the boom days, it is constructed more in the style of the mountain cabin, with steep sloping roof, long porch across the front, and one section of hand-hewn logs. But like the other house, its front yard is bare of grass and littered with the children's "junk," there is no trace of paint, and many window "lights" are broken. The two dark front rooms are crowded with beds. An ailing grandmother sits by the stove coughing out her life and spitting frequently into an old lard can.

The new baby will grow up knowing very little of a home that provides what is not absolutely necessary—rugs and pictures and books, for instance, or furniture made with an eye for beauty, or separate rooms for cooking and eating. His acquaintance with color may begin with the heavy, bright blue wall paper so commonly used here to help keep out the wind. A "picture" to him will be either the picture on the calendar from the store in town or the old faded photograph of his grandparents, hanging on the wall in its large ornate frame. True, he will know what a song is, because his dad whistles and sings any number of mountain songs and ballads, and his mother sings hymns while she rocks him in her arms. And he will know what it is to sleep under handmade quilts of intricate design—(though shiny rayon store-bought quilts are the proud possessions of a few of the younger mothers). He will take them for granted as other children take for granted their beautiful picture books and their rooms with Mother Goose stencils on the delicately tinted walls.

But to this child "the house" will mean chiefly a corner of a bed to sleep in, a warm stove to sit and whittle by when he is cold (perhaps it's a barrel he sits on), and a place where he can run in to get crackers and peanut butter or a cold biscuit when he is hungry—though I do not mean to suggest that the larger concept of "home" will have this limited meaning.

Play space in the house, however, is not so important to him as to a city child. He will spend much of his time outdoors, climbing over the bumping roots of the big tree, helping in the garden in the spring, feeding the chickens, going to the woods with his dad to haul in stovewood, riding the young trees over, cutting hickory whistles, and playing marbles on the hard bare ground in front of his house.

Though one of his grandfathers came here as a very young man to work in the mines and the other was a descendant of the earliest pioneer settler, this child will not grow up in an "ancestral" home. There are not many children in Summerville now who actually live in the homes their grandparents built, for the obvious reason that one roof could not cover them all.

But it is true that there is hardly a child whose grandparents —and aunts and uncles and myriads of cousins—are not still living in Summerville or in a near-by community. In fact, if one sat down to figure it all out, one might find that because of the many intermarriages almost every family has some kind of kinship ties with most of its neighbors.

This new baby, for instance, is coming to a home where he will have a grandmother as well as a father and mother and four older brothers. Just around the corner lives one of his aunts; her daughter, the baby's fourteen-year-old cousin, will frequently come to his house to help take care of him. Another family of seven cousins lives in a house down on the side of the mountain. Their mother dies when our baby is only six months old; some of her children come to stay under his roof for a while, sleeping on a big straw pallet on the floor. His father's uncle, for whom he is named, lives across the tracks, with five grown sons and daughters all in the neighborhood, some of them married, and there is a family of more distant cousins still farther down the road.

Who are these Smiths and their neighbors the Marlowes, Eldridges, Johnsons, Campbells, Kilgores, MacFarlanes, Thomases, Lautzenheisers? It is difficult to get exact knowledge, because those living here now seem to know very little about their ancestors. Many a time when I have asked, "Where did your folks come from?" the answer has been, "Down in the valley." And once when I asked Mr. Kilgore when his people came over here, he said, "Back in Victoria's time, I guess." This family's name wasn't even Kilgore then: "It was handed down to me by my father that our name was Hamilton, but a long time back the Hamiltons got into a quarrel with another family, and when they won the fight they just changed their name to Kilgore." But to judge from the majority of names, which certainly are the "real" names, Summerville people are English, Scotch, and German, and it is probable that their ancestors were among those who came to this country during the great Scotch-Irish and German immigrations of 1720–70 and gradually found their way down to the Southern valleys and mountains from Pennsylvania and the Carolina Piedmont. Or they may have come to Tennessee from Virginia and other Southern coastal states between 1800 and 1850, when decline of prices of cotton and tobacco in the South and exhaustion of the soil sent many Southerners west.

Whichever pioneering stream they stem from, it is obvious that they are people who have an upright if not stern tradition behind them, in spite of the fact that the stock here is undoubtedly somewhat more diluted than in the remote coves of the Southern mountains. That there are some bootleggers still among these people is certainly the case, but the children of even these bootleggers consider themselves outraged if anyone suggests to them that their daddies "drink." "A drunk man ain't got no sense," they say. And it was the grandchild of one of these (a notorious bootlegger, known as the kindest man in the cove) who told me one day solemnly that his daddy had explained to him how "Jesus will burn up the world some day. But only bad people will burn up. Not the good ones." And any child will inform you that "the Boogerman will get you if you work on Sunday."

The very old generation is apt to be more strict than the new, however. I stopped at the Smith house one day when Mrs. Smith's old grandfather was visiting there. He was sitting alone on the porch, singing hymns. I commented on how youthful he looked for a man of 82, and he explained, "It's interest on my good behavior! I had the best mother in the world. She was real close with us. She even knew how to put the oil on! She was always talking to us about what life meant. She told us not to go where we had no business, just leave things alone. You didn't know what might happen there. I never spent a nickel on a show in my life. I never went to a ball game, either, or cared for fox hunting. My pleasures were reading and talking. And I learned about eating from my mother. I learned that good old rough grub is the best thing for you, like onions and potatoes and beans and buttermilk and cornbread—and just watch me eat them!"

The younger Mr. Smith, however, I am sure has been to occasional movies, and takes his children to the Fair and buys them chewing gum and ice cream. But even he still says "Yes sir" to his father, and threatens his children with a whipping if they walk in front of the chair where a guest is sitting.

Mrs. Smith, married fourteen years, is expecting her sixth child. One, she has already buried. Like most of the other young mothers, all she has to do is "expect" without doing much about it. Many a morning when I passed by her house, she was just placidly sitting on the porch. There are seldom regular trips to the doctor—though I believe the Highlander Folk School car did take this mother two or three times to the free clinic at the Oakmont hospital, seven miles away in the adjoining county. As the baby will sleep with its mother, there is no preparation of cribs or other baby paraphernalia. Nor does a bath require special tubs, thermometers, towels, and so on. A small pan of water heated on the stove is all that is necessary. Clothes do have to be made, of course, of white outing flannel with some little embroidered flowers, though there are surely some of the last baby's things left. He is only just three years old now. And there is still the long white silk coat with a collar, for best occasions such as church and funerals. This belonged to some baby in the family many years back.

The little three-year-old boy and his five-year-old brother know nothing about the possibility of a new brother or sister in the family. Nor do the other children, aged seven and nine, unless they have noticed their mother's growing size and have remembered the talk they have heard among the other boys at school. (As Mrs. Bennett down the road was telling me, "George would sometimes sit and stare and stare at me. I'd say something funny to try to liven him up and get him to laughing, but he would just keep on staring in his serious way. As soon as they start to school they begin to learn things!") When the baby comes, the boys will be taken to spend the night at their cousin's, or, if the birth is very easy, they may just sleep through it all in the next room. They will be told in the morning that the doctor brought the baby. The three- and five-year-olds will probably not question the truth of this. In fact, if they are like their little neighbor next door, they will even believe the doctor is being perfectly honest when he comes again later and shows them a place in his suitcase where the baby's fist dug into the lining.

The doctor who is called to the Smith's house is the county health officer. His job does not include delivering babies, but since there are only three other doctors to serve the more than 2,000 families in the county, he seldom fails to answer one of these calls.

The morning the baby was born, I stopped at this house to pick up the two little boys for nursery school as usual, not knowing the new baby had come. The boys came to the door and just looked out at me. I could see that they were not cleaned up for school. I called to them but they couldn't seem to find any words and continued to stand in the doorway just staring at me. I got out of the car to see what was the matter and was met on the porch by a neighbor woman who asked me to come in and see the baby. With a little hesitance I asked, "Does Mrs. Smith want me to?" "Oh, yes!" I learned afterwards that it is customary for practically the whole community to file in and see a new baby on the day of its birth.

There was Mrs. Smith looking as hale and hearty as if the baby had been born a month ago. She was wearing a clean new white nightgown and was lying in a clean bed—a white island in the midst of a very disordered house. I had never before seen this house when it was not immaculately clean, but now with the mother in bed and the father up and off early on his W.P.A. job, the older boys off to school, and the invalid grandmother too weak to do anything but sit all day in her chair by the stove, there was just no one there to do the early morning work. I don't doubt that relatives appeared to help out later in the day. The two little boys were running in and out, sniffling with colds, their clothes, faces, and hands filthy. The neighbor washed the boys and put clean suits on them while I admired the new baby. He appeared to be a large, healthy boy, but when I asked his weight I was told the doctor hadn't weighed him.

The porch door burst open suddenly and in came a little girl from across the road, sneezing and blowing and bringing in a blast of cold air with her. Right up to the bed she went, and leaned over and looked at the baby lovingly, all to the satisfaction of the mother.

When I left with the two little boys, the neighbor woman left also, saying she was so sorry she couldn't stay, her own small baby was alone at home in bed. She would run back and forth all morning, but she *couldn't* stay.

So we left Mrs. Smith beaming, alone in a dirty house with a new baby and a coughing old woman.

This is how life begins for most Summerville children. Sometimes the doctor is not needed—the birth is so easy that the call for him is canceled at the last minute. Occasionally a baby is born in the hospital in Oakmont. But whatever these deviations may be, the baby is sure to find himself immediately the loved darling of his own family and of his host of relatives. He will seldom be out of his mother's arms. And when he is, his sisters and even his brothers will grab him up and cuddle him, for these boys never heard it suggested that it might be sissy for them to fondle and care for babies.

SCENES FROM THE FIRST
THREE YEARS

❀❀❀❀❀❀❀❀❀❀❀❀❀❀❀❀❀❀❀❀❀

I WENT AROUND TO SEE Frances's three months old baby. Frances is seventeen, unmarried, and lives at home with her father and mother, two brothers, and a married sister whose husband and two little children also live with the family in their four-room house.

When I came in, Frances's mother was sitting there rocking the baby. Frances herself was nowhere to be seen. When she appeared presently from the adjoining room, she didn't take the baby from her mother, but sat down near me to talk (or I should say listen to me talk. She is too shy to say much but "Yes'm" to me.) It was her mother who changed the baby's diaper after a little while. And it was her married sister who took the baby next, just to cuddle it and rock it. Finally, when the baby whimpered a little, Frances got up as a matter of course, sat down on the bed, and nursed it without a word.

A baby with three mothers all in the same house, I thought.

I called at Mrs. Clay's at about ten in the morning to find out on which days during the coming week she could cook the soup for the nursery school. I found her sitting beside the stove in the front room. She had just finished bathing and dressing her five months old boy. The "tub"—a small pan of suds for a sponge bath—was still standing on the stove, and a wooden crate turned on end, near by, held the cake of soap. The baby's dirty clothing lay on the floor beside the box.

We sat there for about half an hour, talking and playing with the baby. When he began to fret, Mrs. Clay nursed him a little, saying playfully to him, "It wasn't long ago that you had some!"

"I know a girl down in the valley," she said to me, "who only feeds her baby every four hours. Sometimes before feeding time he will cry and cry. I just couldn't stand that."

"Do you give your baby anything but milk?" I asked.

"No, not very much. Mildred always feeds her baby something whenever she herself sits down to eat, but I never think of it somehow. The other day was the first time I've ever given Billy any solid food. He had some mashed potatoes and chocolate pie."

I asked if the baby was a good sleeper and went to bed early. "He tries to sit up with us in the evenings! He's so crazy over his daddy he stays up with him until he just has to fall asleep."

As I left I told Mrs. Clay that I was driving up to Dyersville. She wanted to come with me to go to the store, so bundled up the baby and called her five-year-old to come along, for the ride, and off we went.

As I walked up to the Smith's gate, I could see through the two open doors into the back yard. Mrs. Smith was out there by the big black washing pot, getting ready to wash the clothes. The oldest son, about ten, was sitting in a rocking chair on the porch, holding the six months old baby in his arms.

"Yes, J.C. takes care of the baby while I wash. He loves to do it. He always grabs up the baby as soon as he gets home from school."

The Community Council meets. Seven or eight members are here tonight, sitting facing one another in a corner of the old cabin called the "community house," formerly an Episcopal mission—the same building, in fact, that housed the nursery school in its early days.

This Community Council, organized with the help of the Highlander Folk School, is an entirely nonpolitical body composed of representatives chosen from each organization in the community (the church, the Parent-Teacher Association, the Union, the young people's club) ; its purpose to find ways of improving community conditions, perhaps seeing that the roads are graded, a needed culvert is built, or that hot lunches are introduced into the school program. Incidentally, the Council also represents an experiment in cooperation, which is far from an easy thing to achieve in a small mountain community where petty rivalries, jealousies, bickerings are apt to loom very large.

The chairman tonight, who is a representative from the Parent-Teacher Association, sits near the kerosene lamp, because she has a letter to read to the group from the Road Commissioner. Just now the Council is working on the problem of getting the county roads improved.

Mrs. Rutledge, from the Sunday School, has brought her nine-year-old daughter with her, to keep her company on the dark walk home. Ophelia sits there beside her mother solemnly and quietly all evening, as though she herself were a regular member of the Council. Mrs. Smith's thirteen-year-old niece, Lizzie, has come too, to keep Mrs. Smith company, and of course the baby (of six and a half months) must go wherever Mrs. Smith goes. He sleeps most of the evening on Lizzie's lap, but as soon as he begins to whimper Mrs. Smith takes him and nurses him until he sleeps again, while the talk goes on of roads and school zone signs and hot lunches for the children.

I had to wait quite a while for Junior one day. His married sister, who seems to take care of her younger brothers and sisters in that household of eight children, as well as of her own baby, finally came out to the car to tell me that "Junior lacks just a little bit of bein' ready now." She brought her baby along—a lively, healthy looking four months old girl, whom I proceeded to admire at once. But the mother (one of the very young mothers of our community, and decidedly of the "younger generation" in tastes and standards) was profuse with apologies. "Oh she's so dirty. She usually gets her bath before this time, but this morning there's been so much to do I just haven't got around to it. She has had her orange juice, though. But look at her ears! She makes such a fuss when I clean them with olive oil."

My introduction to a "modern" baby in Summerville.

The scene is a room in the elementary school building. The county health officer and nurse have stopped by to vaccinate and inoculate. A good many small children have been rounded up, and most of them have come with their mothers.

The doctor works in one corner of the room while anxious, crying children wait on the benches and little chairs along the wall, fearing to be next in turn as they watch the jabbing of each screaming victim.

Three-year-old Marvin's mother holds him on her lap while he receives the shots, but in spite of her presence, and in spite of the doctor's joviality, he cries and clings tightly to her.

Two little girls who have had some of the shots before walk up bravely, calmly.

But here is a seven months old baby. His mother cannot bear to see him go through the process, so when his turn comes, she hands him to the nurse and she herself dashes out to the porch, practically in tears. When it is over she grabs her baby and smothers him with caresses and soothes him with loving, comforting words.

I was sitting on Agnes's porch, chatting with her and her neighbor, young Mildred Moon, who had stopped by with her eight months old baby. Along came the county health nurse who had taken a house for the summer just down the road around the bend.

"Why Mildred Moon," she said, "you go right home and take off all this baby's clothes except her diaper! (The baby had on a full costume of diaper, shirt, slip, dress, shoes and socks.) "You ought to know better—on a hot day like this!"

"But I'm so afraid she'll catch cold," Mildred resisted.

The baby's neck was broken out. Agnes said it was the watery hives, but the nurse laughed and told them there wasn't any such thing. The baby was just too hot, that was all.

"What is she getting to eat these days?"

"Well," Mildred answered, "she eats about what we do—she loves raw onions—"

"What! You ought never give her raw onions, Mildred. Lots of grown people can't eat onions without getting indigestion."

"But she sees us eating them and she likes them so much!"

Josephine attended her first funeral—her grandmother's—at the age of eight months. There were a few present who were even younger than she. In fact, hardly a family in the community failed to turn out with most of its members, young and old, at the funeral of beloved "Aunt Mag."

During the service in the church, during the weeping and preaching and chanting over the open coffin, Josephine sat in a back row in the arms of her fourteen-year-old sister, who had probably chosen a seat apart from her sobbing family as an armor against undignified tears.

Her mother took her and held her when the service was continued out by the grave. There they sat, under the awning provided for the family by the Burial Association, while a light rain fell. But Josephine probably sensed very little of the fact that she was in a strange place, in the midst of a sorrowful gathering. For even there at the graveside, as the coffin was slowly lowered and the mother wept, Josephine was given the comforting breast.

Out on Iva Lee Clark's porch an unusually large crowd of women and girls and babies had gathered. It is common to see at least four women out there, sitting away the hot afternoon in the porch swing, watching the traffic pass on the highway. In fact, this is the major leisure time "activity" of the majority of people in the community, even when their houses do not front the highway. But today there must have been twelve people on Iva Lee's porch, counting the two small babies. They were all neighbors, a number of them relatives. But apparently they had not come together for any special purpose. It was just a happen-so.

A mother and baby were there whom I had not seen before. They had moved fairly recently to the mountain from the valley, to be near their kinfolk.

This afternoon the baby's aunt was holding him. To my aston-

ishment, I saw that this baby, just a year old, was constantly sucking the thumb of his right hand, and with his left hand was twisting a strand of hair on top of his head—the same habit I had seen
in occasional four- and five-year-olds in New York, but never
before in this part of the country.

His mother noticed that I was looking curiously at the baby,
and laughed. "He's always done that, and his brother six years
old does it too, but neither of my girls ever did."

"It's just a habit," explained one of the older women.

They all laughed affectionately at the funny little fellow, as
though they were amused, and no one made any attempt to stop
him or divert him. He went on sucking and twisting happily and
contentedly the whole time I was there—about three quarters of an
hour.

He was not nursed, or I should say given the bottle, during
my visit. Ray is one of the few bottle-fed babies in the community.

We were driving back from town with the mail and the
groceries. It was already dark. As we came to the crossroads, a
man walked into the range of the headlights—a man carrying
a baby dressed in white. My first thought was that the baby must
be ill. But then the lights revealed a cow also, and the whole thing
became clear. Ernest Smith was out driving his cow home, and
he had taken his year-old baby boy with him. We drove past his
house a quarter of a mile farther on. There were members of the
family at home. Apparently Ernest had taken the baby with him
just because he wanted to, not because of necessity.

It was a hot afternoon. I found Mrs. Farmer standing over the
bed where thirteen months old Sarah Jean lay asleep. Mrs. Farmer
was fanning the flies off the child. "She don't get much sleep in
the daytime on account of the flies," she explained.

I had come to see some of the grandmother's quilts. When Mrs.
Farmer stopped fanning the baby and went to open the box
where the quilts were kept, the flies settled so thickly on the

child's face that she started to stir and waken. I picked up the cloth and continued the fanning. I had always wondered why that really beautiful baby had such a tired, listless look.

I scarcely recognized sturdy little Josephine (fifteen months) walking all around the house. When I had last seen her two months earlier she had still been a baby in arms. "Yes, she started right out walking on the day she was thirteen months old," her mother said.

Josephine was still, to a certain extent, a "baby in arms," however. In fact, when I opened the door and walked in that afternoon, I found Mrs. Bennett just sitting in the chair by the stove, placidly rocking the baby, as she had been doing on almost every afternoon of the baby's life when I had happened to call. But Josephine had had a difficult babyhood. She had cried with "colic" for months. Occasionally when I had been there, I had seen Mrs. Bennett give her a sip from the bottle of "cordial" on the shelf, to relieve her discomfort in the way she thought was best. Then, finally, after a trip to the doctor, it was discovered that Josephine just hadn't been getting enough milk. "She was starving, that's all that was the matter with her." She was given canned milk, to supplement the breast feeding, and the "colic" disappeared.

Now, at fifteen months, she was a chubby, big little girl, and even wearing "breeches."

"Look what Josephine's wearing!" her mother proudly showed me. "This is only the second day she's had them on." Josephine promptly demonstrated that she did not yet understand the intricacies of "breeches," but her mother was patient and gentle, though at the same time feeling the need of shaming her. "Why Josephine, look what you done, you wet your breeches. Look at that, um, um,—and right here in front of Miss Lewis." Then aside to me, "She usually tells me when she has to go, but it's only her second day and she feels strange with you here."

The wet breeches were sent right out to the big sister who was doing the washing in the yard, and Josephine, after roaming about for a while, climbed back up into her mother's lap for a comfortable bit of rocking.

"Yes, she's getting to be a big girl now. You can't scare her any more about the dog, to make her go off to sleep. We never tried to make her think the dog would get her, or anything like that, but when she'd get restless and scrammish around in the bed we'd say, 'Listen to the dog bark!' And she'd just scrooge down under the covers and lie so still, and go back to sleep. But she's too used to hearing the dog bark now.

"And sometimes I even have to get cross and put her off by herself. Now Ethel and Grant (Josephine's sister and father), they just want to let her go ahead and do anything she pleases, but I think it's better not to do that, in the long run."

I heard that there was a family living back in the woods off the road, and that they had children of nursery school age. As I walked up the path toward their cabin, there was a great scampering. Three little boys ranging from three to eight in age leaped into the trees like monkeys. Each one was gnawing on a raw sweet potato.

I stepped up to the open door of the cabin and looked in. All of the Summerville homes are crowded and small, but usually have at least two rooms. This was just a one-room cabin, roughly built and never finished off. Cracks between the floor boards must have been letting in a good deal of the chilly October air.

The cabin was furnished with the barest minimum—two double beds for the six people, a cookstove, a table and a chair or two, with a number of barrels for additional chairs. There were shelves for food near the stove.

Mrs. Ladd was sitting in the rocker holding a beautiful, sturdy little girl who looked to be about two years old. We talked about the nursery school and about the children. The oldest boy came in, found a cold biscuit, and dashed out again. When Mrs. Ladd began to nurse the child on her lap, I asked her age. She was twenty months old. "I know I shouldn't still be nursing her, but . . ."

She didn't finish the sentence. She didn't need to.

"Miss Lewis," said Edna to me one morning at the nursery school, "did you know that Wiley's baby burned up last night?"

"What Wiley, Edna? I didn't know they had a baby. Do you mean it really burned up so that it's dead now?"

"No, hit ain't dead but hit's all burned up."

I never did get this story straight. I think Edna had been hearing bits of conversation which she had put together the wrong way. Perhaps she had heard about the burning of Jimmy Marlowe—or there may very well have been another I did not know of. Falling against the hot stove is a very common accident here.

I decided to stop in and see sixteen months old Jimmy, and find out if his burn was more serious than I had heard.

I found him with a badly blistered hand and half his face disfigured. His mother, holding him in her arms, cheerily told me that "Hit's a lot better now. I put salve on hit right away, and when we carried him to the doctor he said I'd done just right. Yes'm, he stumbled while he was getting down off the chair and fell right against the stove."

I stopped in at King's on Sunday afternoon to leave a message. I must have arrived in the midst of a meal—or possibly it was just a mid-afternoon snack. The four-year-old boy was sitting in a rocker by the stove eating a biscuit, and to judge from the peels on the floor around the stove, he had recently had an orange too (from the surplus commodities furnished by the Public Welfare Department). The nineteen months old baby, all cleaned up for Sunday in a white dress, was holding a biscuit in one hand and a greasy sausage ball in the other, as he sat on his mother's lap. He made very slow headway with either of these; in fact, he kept dropping large pieces of both on the floor. His mother, with patience and good humor, just picked the pieces up each time and put them down on the sewing machine, which happened to be within easy reach of her chair.

"Who can that little boy be?" I thought to myself as we drove past the Tates' on our daily trip to collect the children for the nursery school. A little boy in overalls was out on the porch. It wasn't Clarence and it wasn't George (I knew both of those boys well), and it wasn't the baby—but yes, it *was* the baby, the big two-year-old boy who heretofore had worn nothing but a short dress, sometimes with but more often without underpants, as is the common custom in the community in the case of both girls and boys under three.

Leander in overalls! Graduation from babyhood.

I was doing the sweeping and straightening up at the nursery school in the afternoon. The little two-year-old girl who lived in the house next door was out playing in the back yard with her cousin, who was there for the day. They began to pull on something, each wanting it and neither willing to give it up. I heard Geneva's mother calling out directions for behavior from the window in a shrill voice, but the little impasse continued. In a moment the mother was out there, switching her child's legs sharply with a razor strap, and screeching admonitions I could not make out.

A special event at the Duncans' house. The nursery school teacher and the community worker from the Highlander Folk School were coming for supper. That meant a table cloth, and a meal when everyone sat down together and especially good food was served.

But there weren't enough seats to go around. The three little boys stood at one side of the table to eat, giggling self-consciously now and then, but for the most part silently consuming saucer after saucer of delicious salmon cakes, potato salad, corn, peas, biscuits, and banana custard. Little Ella, nearly three, sat before her plate in a state of awe, never saying a word, eating practically nothing. No one tried to make her eat; she was just left alone to stare at the unaccustomed scene.

Even the littlest baby ("the least one"), five months old, was there too, of course, wriggling and crying on her mother's lap at one end of the table, making it practically impossible for Mrs.

Duncan to eat anything. But after all, there was nothing else to be done—no pen, no crib, no carriage to lay the baby in. Just as soon as the meal could be called finished, Mrs. Duncan moved a few feet away from the table to the stove, where she sat and nursed the baby till it fell asleep.

The schoolhouse was jammed with people of all ages, for our Christmas play (put on free of charge by the P.T.A.). To be sure, Christmas was a few weeks past, but late was better than never, and everyone realized it had been very difficult to round up all of the "actors"—Summerville housewives—for rehearsals.

There we were, going strong. I was the little girl talking to my mother (P.T.A. president) about Santa Claus. A baby in the audience began to wail. I raised my voice, thinking surely this will last only a minute. Surely the baby's mother will take him out to the porch till he stops. But on and on and on went the wailing, and on and on went the actors, battling against it.

I learned afterwards, when I had been to other plays and evening meetings, that babies are not taken out when they cry. One just accepts their presence and puts up with the noise, as one puts up with other inevitable difficulties such as poor light and drafts in the cold corners of the rooms. A baby is a baby, and of course he cries sometimes, but that's no reason why he or his mother should miss what's going on.

To my surprise, Buddy had his little sister carefully and proudly by the hand as he came out to the nursery school car. Barbara was only two and a half (I had set the nursery school age at three), and usually ran out to the gate each day to see Buddy off. But here she was all dressed up, even wearing underwear, and climbing into the car with Buddy.

I knew that her mother had already gone off to work. I could see her invalid father standing behind the screen door, looking out to see that all was well. Perhaps he would come out and explain. But no, it was the eight-year-old daughter who came running around from behind the house to make the request: "Miss Lewis, mother said would you care for Barbara to come to school today? She wants to go so bad. And if she's any trouble she won't go tomorrow."

So Barbara journeys out into the world, with a five-year-old protector affectionately guarding her and instructing her in the ways of nursery school behavior. "Barbara, do you need to go to the toilet?" he suddenly thinks to ask her softly in the middle of the morning. And when she sits up on her cot during rest time, he whispers to her gently that she must lie down. He leaves his play with the older boys to come and see what she is doing. When he finds her playing house, he gets busy and makes mud pies for her.

It has been a big day for Barbara. Most of her life has been spent within the confines of her own house and yard. Peering out between the boards of the fence, she has seen the neighbors passing by on Branchtown Road. An occasional car, an occasional truck, horses and cows and hogs—all of these she has seen pass.

But her own journeying has probably been almost completely limited to the walk on Sunday with her family over to her grandmother's house, about a mile away. She has been about the community somewhat less than many of the other children, because her father has been ill for a long time and her mother has had to work away from home.

There have been strange and somewhat terrifying new sights and sounds on this day at the nursery school: a playful, barking dog jumping up on the children, the roaring motorcycle of the boy next door, an outhouse with a deep dark hole which she is supposed to use, and a man with a camera. ("He is pointing a *gun* at me!" must have been Barbara's terrified thought as she clung to me.)

But now the day is past, and the car brings Barbara back to her familiar home. Buddy helps her off the running board. As I drive away, I can see through the mirror that her father has come out to meet her, his baby who has suddenly grown up. He holds out his arms and she rushes into them.

Babyhood in Summerville, in fact, means a time of comfort and cuddling in someone's loving arms. For months it means milk at the breast whenever you want it, as well as other food too, almost any other food that others are eating, from onions to chocolate pie, if you want it.

In short, many of the "deprivations" that a baby undergoes in other parts of our country are unknown to the Summerville baby. He is not left at home when his parents go out; he does not have to be torn away and tucked into bed before he feels sleepy; he is present when guests come; even as a small baby it is right and proper that he should participate in life's fundamental solemnities, such as buryings; and for the majority the matter of toilet training is scarcely a serious hurdle. Furthermore, he is dressed as a baby, and nursed and cuddled, for a good long time, with no one expecting him or wanting him to grow up. He is surrounded by protective, adoring brothers and sisters, and in many cases there are even several "mothers" available at almost any time, for care and comfort.

And if he wants to suck his thumb and twist his hair, no one is going to try to stop him or even worry a whit over him. His parents aren't aware of many "problems" in connection with him, and hence the atmosphere of his home is not charged with this kind of tension.

But babyhood, which is in so many ways a haven of delight from his own point of view, has its pitfalls, especially from the point of view of the observer, who sees him sometimes burning his tender skin on the stove that is so prominent in every cabin, and sees those responsible for him laying the foundations of lack of energy through failure or inability to provide proper feeding, clothing, and sufficient time or place for sleep.

He himself, of course, is unaware of these sandy physical foundations, so strong and comforting are the psychological ramparts on all sides of him. He does learn at least one or two fears very early, however, notably fear of the doctor. And after he is old enough to walk around and get into trouble, there may be fear of threatened whippings or spankings to reckon with, and perhaps fear of barking dogs at night, if he is not "good."

Even as a mere baby he begins to absorb the feeling for "proper

behavior" that his parents will try to implant in him in much
larger doses later on. When he is beginning to wear "breeches,"
toward the end of babyhood, he learns that it is shameful to wet
them; if he quarrels and grabs toys from the little cousin who is
visiting, he may get his legs switched, or get "put off by himself"
—by his mother, even if not by his father. True, because of this
inconsistency, he may find it impossible to take some of this discipline very seriously. But the actual behavior of his parents he
will take seriously and begin to copy. When his mother can grind
out only "Yes'm" and "No'm" in the presence of the outlander,
when his father respectfully says "Yes sir" to his grandfather,
such behavior becomes an accepted part of his world, as accepted
as the love his family gives him, as the dangerous hot stove in the
middle of the room, as the place that is his as a member of a community even though he is just a baby.

THE PRE-SCHOOL YEARS

❀❀❀❀❀❀❀❀❀❀❀❀❀❀❀❀❀❀❀❀❀❀

WAYNE EDWARD had not been to nursery school for several days. His little sister Virginia was coming as usual, bouncing out to the gate as she heard our car approaching, holding her jar of milk in one hand and a bunch of flowers for teacher in the other. Sometimes Wayne Edward would be there at the gate, too, but obviously not cleaned up for school.

"Why aren't you coming, Wayne Edward?" I would ask.

"Don't want to. Good-by, Virginia!" was the cheery answer.

I knew that occasionally Wayne Edward stayed home for something like a hog-killin', but he had never been absent for days, like this. I went around to see his mother one afternoon to find out what the trouble was.

She explained that her husband had been laid off W.P.A., and the boy wanted to stay home too, to be with him.

"I don't want to force him to go to school. He might get a contrary spell and then you'd have a difficult time with him."

"Does he often get contrary spells?" I asked.

"No, he's a right good boy and never has given me no trouble, and that's why I don't want to start in making him contrary now. And anyway hit wouldn't do no good to force him to go to kindergarten. He wouldn't like it then and there'd be no point in it, just like you can't force a child to go to grammar school. If he ain't willin' to go then he won't learn nothin'."

One morning about a week later the children all rushed to the fence of the play yard at the nursery school to watch a horse and wagon pass on the highway. Who should it be but Wayne Edward and his daddy, the boy in the driver's seat, holding the reins, looking for all the world like a small edition of the man sitting beside him.

When we took Virginia home later that day, we passed them on the road again. They had left the wagon at grandpa's and now were taking the horse to the barn. The little boy was riding, the big jovial man walking.

"He'll be back at school when I go back to work," he called out. "I can't get rid of him now! He wants to stick right with me!"

Julia lives in a log cabin, one of the oldest houses in the community. In fact, it probably belongs not really to Summerville, but to an even poorer neighborhood on the outskirts, called the "Cove," a district considered by Summerville residents as decidedly in a lower social class, so I gather.

The story goes that this old cabin is built on the county line, half in our county, half in the adjoining one, and they say the original owners used to move back and forth into different halves of the house when the tax collector came around.

At present the half of the house in our county is in a state of real ruin—falling in and open to the weather and the weeds. Julia and her three older sisters and mother and father live in the one good room that is left, in the other county.

I have noticed that Julia is often left in the care of the little sisters, seven and eleven. Her mother sometimes accompanies her father to the woods to cut bugwood (used commercially for its alcoholic content), and often seems to have business in town at the grandmother's. When I bring Julia home at noon, I frequently have to leave her at her cousin's up the road; if there is anyone at her own home, more often than not it is just one of the little sisters. These girls seem to go to school very irregularly. It's a long walk from where they live, and perhaps they lack clothes. Then, too, there is the washing to help with, and sometimes eleven-year-old Margaret is the one who has to cook her daddy's dinner.

On this day, evidently mother is not at home, and the youngest sister has been left to get Julia "ready" for school. The little girl comes out to the car looking exactly like some old frowzledhaired doll (a very sweet-faced doll) that a three-year-old child has tried to dress, with that three-year-old contentment at merely draping and half tying. Her dirty, flowered cotton dress belongs to an older sister and comes down to her bare feet. In the effort to make the dress a little shorter, a belt that is a ragged strip cut from overall cloth is tied in a knot around the waist. There was once a zipper opening down the front, but it is all torn out now, and the dress gapes open clear to the child's naked stomach. I pin it with the only safety pin at my disposal—a huge one—adding, unfortunately, the last three-year-old touch.

Julia is clutching a cold, burned biscuit in one hand and two spring onions, just pulled from the garden, in the other. "Is this her breakfast?" I asked the little sister who helps her into the car. "No'm. She just goes and gets a biscuit when she wants to, like I do."

I saw the mother next day. "I gave Pauline a whipping for letting Julia go to school looking like such a hog," she said.

The room was filled with neighbors who had come in to sit with the bereaved family till the coffin was brought in for the little baby. Both men and women were there, and babies in arms. And small children from the neighborhood felt free to wander in and out whether or no their parents were there.

Presently the men brought the little wooden coffin. Two neighbor women, who seemed self-appointed, stepped right up and took charge, laying cotton batting on the bottom and arranging a sheet inside. Then they lifted the body from the table near by, where it had been lying beneath a white cover, and laid it in the coffin. Everyone crowded around, children and all, and wept softly for a few minutes, before the men took up the little box and carried it to the car outside.

Up at the graveyard the coffin was opened while the preacher from town read from the Bible and said prayers. All of the people stood in a semicircle at a little distance, and wept miserably. I noticed that four or five curious little boys, two of them my pupils, had crowded up close to the open coffin, and were standing there solemnly staring at what must have been a somewhat terrifying sight—a small baby in a thin white dress, exposed to the bitter November cold, lying there with half-open eyes, utterly motionless.

At school one day I was talking with the children about the "strongest thing in the world." We were trying to think of something that might be stronger than steel. Five-year-old Buddy suddenly realized that he knew of something stronger, and insisted that "Jesus is the strongest thing in the world."

Buddy: "He made the whole world in three days. He's going to destroy the whole world again, too. He's going to burn up the mean people."

Wayne Edward: "That old Boogerman is!"

Buddy: "That old Boogerman ain't done it! *Jesus* will. He's going to catch the ground on fire, but he won't burn it all."

Edna: "Has Jesus got matches?"

Wayne Edward: "Hit ain't cold a bit up in heaven, is it?"

No doubt about it, something was wrong with the car; the community's well-known gasoline thief must have been busy the night before. There I was, on the highway, with seven or eight children who were about two miles from their homes. Nothing to do but get out and walk to each child's house in turn, with the hot and hungry little troupe trailing along with me from house to house.

But my oldest boy, who was nearly six, realized as well as I did that it was too much of a walk for our frail little Marvin. Of his own accord, he hoisted him up and carried him pick-a-back as far as he could.

We heard that the doctor had given her up. And looking at her it was hard to believe that she could recover, such a shrunken, pale little mite of a girl.

They had carefully propped her up in a big rocking chair, and were giving her all the loving care that it was possible to give in a two-room shack crowded with small children.

As we stood there talking with the family, the mother kept gently stroking the hair on the child's forehead. When we left, we took the father to town with us. He didn't touch the little girl, but said to her with great gentleness: "Don't you cough like that while I'm gone, sister."

"Miss Lewis, we went to the Fair last night and I rode on the live horses and the horses that weren't alive . . . and I had a hamburger and I gave half to Barbara but she didn't eat it and she gave it back to me and I ate it . . . and we had ice cream cones . . . and there was a lady so fat that six yards of goods had to go into a dress for her, that's what daddy said . . . and I rode on the live horses."

This was Buddy's morning "report" as he climbed into the car with Barbara. Always he was eager to tell me something, but today it couldn't be told in a sentence, and he recurred to it all during the morning; how the whole family had borrowed Grant Tate's car the night before and had gone up to the County Fair in Dyersville, the big event of the year.

"And there was a little monkey there, just as big as this (measuring from the tip of his middle finger up to his shoulder), and his feet looked like hands. And I rode on the live horses and the horses that weren't alive."

Little three-year-old Barbara didn't have a thing to say about the Fair. She just went sleepily and quietly through the morning.

A grandmother, eighty years old: "Hit cured the Moon children when they had the thrash—every one o' them. Just get old Mr. Brown's shoe and put water in the toe of it. Then tip it so the water runs into the heel. Tip it nine times, mind you, and when you rinse out your mouth with that water, hit'll cure you if anything will!"

It was about four o'clock in the afternoon. Mrs. Henderson was in the neat little kitchen preparing potatoes for the five o'clock supper. The two youngest children, my pupils, were playing at the house across the road, but came rushing home when they saw our car stop by their house. Into the kitchen they burst, grabbing up hunks of raw potato to chew on, as a matter of course, while they perched on the table to listen to us.

Their father came home from his W.P.A. job a few minutes later. No sooner had he laid his dinner pail and a small brown sack down on a low shelf than the little boy flew at both of them.

From the sack he pulled a generous slice of cheese, no doubt intended for the evening meal, and began to bite right into it, probably showing off a little bit in front of his teacher.

His mother went over to him and quietly but firmly took it away from him, saying, "I've had just about enough of this."

But before putting the cheese up on the shelf she cut off what looked to me to be a huge slice for each of the children.

Peace reigned then. Mrs. Henderson went on preparing supper, while the children contentedly munched their cheese and raw potatos.

Mr. Henderson sat there and talked about his job—how he had to get up at 4:30 when he was working down at the sand-cut in order to get there on time. Suddenly he remembered to tell his little boy, "Son, I saw your calf loose when I came in. You better go out and tie her up."

The boy just answered that he didn't care if she was loose, but no doubt he went to hunt for her when we left.

Scene: *Lunch time at the nursery school:*
J.B. (Laughing and joking and talking a string of nonsense):
   "I'll cut off your tail!"
Ina Lee (Righteously, quoting an admonition heard at home):
   "J.B. Farmer, you're at the table!"

When we stopped for five-year-old Elsie May in the morning, we found her out in her yard beside a big tub, surrounded by dozens of empty fruit jars.

"Elsie ain't goin' this morning," her mother called from the doorway. "She's stayin' home to wash out the jars for me. My hand's too big to get inside 'em and hers is just right."

Elsie was working away. She smiled and waved good-by to us cheerily.

It was a very hot morning. Agnes, pregnant, barefoot, and wearing the little white cap she always wore around the house, was just sitting in a rocker in the shade of the big tree by the back door. "At the turn of the day I don't feel so well," she had explained to me before. Her mother was out there, too, peeling potatoes for dinner. When Agnes saw that I was opening the gate and coming in, she called to Ina Lee to run and get a chair for me. I don't know just how the child did it, but she had the chair out there before I had finished fastening the gate.

It was a leisurely and pleasant hour we spent there under the tree, talking about the President, the W.P.A. and the good Lord.

Ina Lee went off to her playhouse up against the wall of the chicken house, and busied herself with a doll and some dishes. Occasionally she looked over our way, but did not intrude or try to get our attention. For a while she even sat in her little rocker with her back to us, singing to herself as she tried to scrape some gum off her hands.

Presently she began to look for an old piece of cloth her big sister had given her. She couldn't find it, and wandered around among us, talking about it. Finally it was the grandmother who told her to go off and "hush." But as she started to walk through the kitchen door, her mother called after her gently, "Sugar Pie, go around to the front door. Ethel just mopped the kitchen."

Ina Lee was back soon with her cloth, and played happily off by herself again.

I scarcely noticed when she brought her rocker and placed it close beside her mother's. She wanted to practice writing her ABC's, and had found a pencil and scrap of paper. Without talking or interfering with her mother's conversation she struggled away to form a few letters, handing the paper up to her mother occasionally for correction and new models to copy. Agnes always looked with interest at the paper, and wrote the models as the child wished, while she talked on about how the Lord had tried her when Ina Lee's heel was so bad, but her faith had carried her through, and how last week Aunt Ellie had taken her for a ride to Montvale, 20 miles away, the first time in all her thirty-six years on the mountain that she had been to that town.

It was one of those warm Indian summer October days. As we drove up to Virginia's house, at about 12:30, the scene on her porch was a perfect picture of lazy ease. There was old Granny in the rocker, just sittin' rockin'. But no rocker was comfortable enough for Virginia's big dad. He lay stretched out on the porch with his head resting on a chair tipped to just the right angle. And there was little Wayne Edward, too, at full length just like his dad, except that he had found a softer head-rest on his dad's "old fat belly."

Soaking up the sun.

The union of the unemployed and relief workers, to which most of the men in the community belonged at that time, had a campfire for their families in the field back of Jim Priest's house. A beautiful big bonfire on an autumn night, and coffee and sandwiches and marshmallows and songs, and a talk by the beloved square-dance caller and teacher from the Folk School, who had been away for two years and now was back in the neighborhood for a few days.

All of the seven Smiths were there, all of the eleven Marlowes, all of the six Hills and all of the seven Farmers and their cousins —though two of the littlest ones couldn't stay awake and slept inside the house. Perhaps there were fifty or sixty people in all. It was a quiet crowd, sitting around watching that beautiful blaze. Even the children sat there still. Once Martin began to wrestle a little with Horace, but his dad, on the alert to make his boy behave in public, promptly called out to him to stop. Later two children picked up burning sticks and were reprimanded with such alacrity as I had seldom seen here before. But that was all. Peaceful, quiet.

The older children passed the marshmallows around, and were especially considerate to see that the younger ones got their share.

Ernestine: "Miss Lewis, I slept with mother last night. You know why? 'Cause daddy was drunk."

We were bouncing along over the rough road down in the "Cove," taking Julia home from school. About halfway we picked up her big fourteen-year-old sister, who was walking back from town with groceries. Betty was sucking a huge lollypop that had come off its stick.

"Give me some candy!" was three-year-old Julia's greeting.

Betty immediately took the candy out of her mouth and handed it to Julia, without an instant's hesitation.

(Was such consideration due to my presence, I wondered?)

It was March, and already warm and springlike. Mrs. Tate was in the side room, which was never used in winter, sweeping it out and peeling the old torn paper off the walls and ceiling. "Ain't it pretty weather!" she said. "I'm goin' to enjoy it as fast as I can because I'm afraid it won't last."

The two oldest boys, three and six, were outside helping their dad get the ground ready for a garden.

"Yes, the boys are just crazy over Sam, and love nothing better than to help him. They even fight to sleep with him, so we have them take turn about, one sleeps with me one night and then with Sam the next night. The only way I get Leander (the baby) to sleep with me is to tell him the Big Black Nigger will get him if he don't."

I went over in the afternoon to see why John had not come to school. There he was sitting on his mother's lap, not on his own porch but next door, where his mother's sister lived. Hair cutting was going on out there, and everyone had gathered around to watch.

I asked why John had not come to school and was surprised to hear that he had been very sick that day, sick to his stomach. In fact, "he turned as blue as indigo in the face this morning," his mother claimed. He looked pale and was lying listlessly in his mother's lap, but apparently keeping him in bed was a thought that never entered his mother's head.

A father: "Why, J.B. and Anna can't hardly wait to go to nursery school in the morning. Right after they get up from the table they go down to the spring and get their pail of water, and set it on the stove, and from then on keep pesterin' their mother to wash 'em so they can go."

Some of the children had been telling me that they had been down in the valley to hear Brother Adams preach. Every now and then Ernestine would burst into lusty song, "When the roll is called up yonder." But when I asked Ina Lee what the preacher had said, she had no answer except, "He played a git-tar."

Then Brother Adams came to Summerville for a two weeks' revival. All other meetings in the community were suspended during that time—no use trying to compete with the revival.

The little community church (formerly Methodist) was packed every night with men, women, children, whole families, many of them people who seldom went to church at any other time during the year. For there were those in Summerville who, though they observed Sunday strictly and never doubted the truths of the Bible, yet did not frequent the churches, and might tell you philosophically that as they saw it, "Religion is like building a house. You keep on building it all the time till you die, and when you're dead, it's built."

Ina Lee's grandmother brought her to school one day during the revival (handing me a banana to give her if she got hungry, because she hadn't wanted any breakfast).

"Brother Adams is preachin' over at old Howard Smith's at ten o'clock this mornin'. There ain't much hope left for the pore old man. I wish you could go this mornin'. And I wish you could a' heerd him last night! There's three of us at our house thankin' the Lord!"

I went to hear Brother Adams on Sunday afternoon.

Someone had told me that the Reverend had spent two years in the penitentiary before he was "saved." His deeply furrowed forehead and his shifting glance (he kept looking out of the windows and at his watch as he paced back and forth on the platform), made it not hard to believe.

Sure enough, he did play the guitar, and had a mixed quartet with him too. During one of the opening songs the soprano lost out entirely. Brother Adams looked around at her with an annoyed and almost disgusted expression, but rewarded her with a beaming smile when she finally boomed out the right notes.

Then came the testimonials and the sermon, with stories of daddies and little children and gray-haired mothers, and the prisoner who was about to die, kissing his wife and babe for the last time, all because he had gone the wrong way, the way of liquor and sin.

Now Brother Leonard here (in the quartet) had just been saved from a life of sin after his own brother had been shot down recently in the honky-tonk. (At this point Brother Leonard rushes out of the church in tears.)

Come forward now, good people. Is it worth a prayer to be able to shake your daddy's hand in heaven?

"Almost persuaded," they sing. Are you going to see your dear old mother again up there?

No one goes forward to be saved. I expect that this whole congregation has been saved before, except for the babies and little boys and girls of nursery school and school age. Well, they will have plenty of opportunity later. Brother Adams comes every spring.

Julia came to school with a little can I recognized as a snuff can, one of her mother's old empty ones, I presumed.

"Does your mother dip snuff?" was a question heard at the

nursery school one day. From almost all the children, the answers came, "Yes, mine does." "Yes." "My mother does."

To my amazement, Julia came up during the morning and showed me not only the contents of the can but the lump of snuff she had placed in her mouth under her lower lip.

Somewhat aghast and finding myself in a situation I had never had to face before, I said, "You don't *like* that, do you?"

"Yes," was the calm and matter-of-fact answer, as she turned away and went back to her play.

I went over to young Ethel Clay's at about eight o'clock in the morning, on an errand for the Folk School.

Mrs. Clay's three-room log cabin was in great disorder at that time of day, and she herself was not yet cleaned up. She flew around pulling drawers open in the desk in the main room and in the dresser in the bedroom, hunting for this and that, and always appealing to her five-year-old daughter for help, almost as though she were a sister of equal age.

"Elsie May, where's my comb? I had it to comb your hair this morning. Elsie, do you know where mother's cream is? My face is drawing up—help me look for it, Elsie."

Frances, the little seventeen-year-old girl who came to the nursery school each morning to help me, usually brought her three-year-old nephew along with her. On this particular day he did not come. She explained that he was still asleep when she left and she couldn't wake him.

"Does he go to bed too late?" I asked.

"Yes'm, sometimes he does. He sleeps with me and hates to go to bed before I do."

Mealtime conversation at the nursery school, between four- and five-year-olds:

Me: "Buddy, is your father working now?"

Buddy: "Yes."

Marvin: "How much does he earn?"

Buddy: (Unable to answer).

J.B.: "My father's working down in the valley."

Buddy: "That's where we thought he was a-workin'. We was talkin' about him at home. Dick's (the eleven-year-old brother) workin' in town."

Marvin: "Is he deliverin' papers?"

Buddy: "No, mamma cut him off of that."

Marvin: "Why did she?"

Buddy: "Because he wasn't gettin' no pay."

Three families withdrew their children from nursery school the week that Caroline Foster was assigned to help me under the N.Y.A. "I couldn't trust her with my children, she don't like children," is the only explanation they could give me, but through friends who knew the situation thoroughly I learned that there were deeper underlying prejudices, old family prejudices, as well as a rather general feeling among many in the community that this Foster family held itself off. "They don't have nothin' to do with people, and anyway Caroline don't need the work." True, some of the young people in this family had been unusually successful in getting good jobs away from Summerville. Caroline, who had spent some time with one of her married sisters in another state, had very attractive, though not expensive, clothes. Did Summerville people resent what they considered was the somewhat superior status of the Foster family? Or was there a real aloofness on the part of the family which was unacceptable to the community's standards of neighborliness and hospitality and the feeling that none-shall-be-better-than-others?

However it was, there was nothing I could do about it, in spite of my belief that Caroline was in reality a very capable, if not superior, young girl. The mothers were as friendly to me as ever, but firm in their stand against the girl: "I've spoken my mind, and that's my privilege, to have my own opinion. That's about the only privilege we do have around here!"

So, five children were withdrawn at one fell swoop. I began

to go about the community looking for others to fill the gap. One day I stopped in to see young Mary Eldridge, perhaps the youngest mother in Summerville, certainly the youngest looking. I sat there in the kitchen watching her knead up the dough for the supper biscuits. Slight, frail, her beautiful fluffy brown hair falling down to her shoulders, she looked no more than sixteen. It was hard to believe she was the mother of the four-year-old boy who was playing around the kitchen steps.

We talked softly because her husband was asleep in the next room—he had to sleep in the daytime because his was an all-night job at a service station in Piedmont.

"I'm afraid I couldn't let Buddy go to nursery school," Mary said. "I don't know what I'd do without him. Last week he went down to the valley for an hour and a half and I nearly went crazy. And anyway, I'm sure his daddy wouldn't let him go. When he went off to work the other day, he said to me, 'Whatever you do, watch out for that boy!' "

Wayne Edward announced to me one day that his mother didn't let him go across the road to play with Junior Layne any more.

"Why not?" I asked.

"So I won't hear him cuss," was the righteous answer.

I had to smile to myself. Wayne Edward had been hurling the cuss words around as naturally and as frequently as most of the other children. It was impossible for me to believe that children who cussed in the matter-of-fact way these did were not exposed to it in their own homes.

In fact, just the next day some of the children began to talk about whether or not their parents cussed. Wayne Edward was among those who said they did, while Buddy volunteered the information that "My daddy and mother cuss all the time whenever they get mad. They were mad last night. Mother said daddy wouldn't let her eat. But I never heard daddy say nothin' about she couldn't eat."

The children were getting into an argument about whether or not grown-ups run.

Buddy: "Why yes, they run. A man ran around the house once when he was trying to kill my daddy with a rock."

I found Mrs. Priest at home alone that afternoon, alone, that is, except for the banty hen keeping her company. "The banty won't lay nowhere but in the house," she apologized.

I hadn't been there two minutes, however, before the three youngest children (three to six), appeared out of the woods and began to peek in at the door. I knew all of these children well. They had all been in my school at various times and I frequently called at their house. Their father was one of the leaders of the community, and the parent who was always showing up at the nursery school to find out if he could help me in any way, particularly with repair work around the place.

But in spite of my familiarity with the family, my visits to the home always threw the children into a state of mixed shyness and excitement; they wanted to get my attention and play with me, but were consumed with embarrassment. The two little boys began by coming up to the doorway with paper sacks on their heads, quickly leaping out of sight as soon as I looked. Then they grew bolder and began to make quick dashes through the house, in at the front, out at the back, blowing whistles as they ran, and pointing toy pistols at me and saying "Bang!"

"Stop that. Put that down," Mrs. Priest would say.

But the barrage of noise and dashing continued.

The little girl hid behind the door and began to croak loudly, "Cawdee Lewis! Cawdee Lewis!"

"Be quiet!" from her mother.

The only response to that was an excited dash over to the bunch of carrots I had brought with me from the school garden. She grabbed one up, though she was promptly told to Bring That Back, and dashed outside with it. I never saw it again.

The climaxing act took place as I was preparing to leave. The little boys came to the door dragging along with them a huge dead copperhead snake. "These children do just about everything but behave," Mrs. Priest said, in despair.

Mrs. Bennett, reproving Ina Lee in my presence: "Ina Lee, don't you say 'Yeah!' That's what colored people say—some colored people. You say 'Yes Ma'am'!"

I took the nursery school children over to the Folk School to see some of the marvels of modern life such as faucets, bathtubs, electric stoves, typewriters, and pianos.

Edna and Buddy tried the typewriter eagerly, but J.B. could not bring himself to touch this strange thing. And when I placed Julia on the piano stool, she sat stiffly as though frozen, unable to touch the keys. In a moment she climbed down and drew close to me, hanging on to my dress.

Billy Norwood is a child against whom there is some discrimination on the part of the other children. Billy lives in a mere shed with his father and eight-year-old sister. His mother died a year ago of a miscarriage.

Perhaps the other children realize that Billy is ragged and unkempt and dirty (getting him ready for school is a process that sometimes takes place right out in the middle of the road, as sister Bessie chases him down with a grimy-looking wet rag with which she attempts to wipe off his face and arms while he struggles). "Billy, your face is black as tar!" the children are apt to remark as he climbs into the car.

Perhaps some of the discrimination is just due to the fact that he lives down in the Cove. But certainly part of it, at least in Wayne Edward's eyes, is because Billy does "terrible" things.

"You know my mother's dresser drawers, Miss Lewis? That Billy Norwood went all through them! And he stole my two little trucks."

When Evelyn came out to the car, she had an apple in one hand and a blackberry jam sandwich in the other. Her mother, who never fails to come out to the car with her, explained that "our folks have come up for the day and we've been so busy we haven't had any chance to get breakfast yet, so Evelyn's taking along a little something to eat."

Evelyn is the frailest looking child in the nursery school, one of the very few children in the community whom a photographer of a poverty-stricken area would be sure to pick out to illustrate "undernourishment." A faculty member from the Highlander Folk School discovered Evelyn's destitute family living in a barn a number of years ago, when Evelyn herself was a very small baby —and a very sick one.

The Folk School people and a group of neighbors got together and put up the tiny log cabin where the family of six now lives.

Paul William is six now, and started to grammar school this year, so perhaps this story doesn't really belong here under the pre-school years. But I don't believe that Paul William's smoking has just cropped up this year. According to reports from other children, he was an old hand at it even at five.

"I've hired him to stop, but it don't do no good," his mother said that night as the little boy rolled, lighted, and smoked a cigarette with the air of a seasoned smoker.

"Throw that away, brother!" but brother paid no attention.

His dad sat there watching him, rather enjoying the spectacle.

"Now ain't you a sight! Ain't you smart," he said.

Brother got up and put the stub in the stove when he had finished. Paul William is the boy whose mother told me once that "He'd find a way to get ahold of what he wanted even if I hid it up in the beams of the house."

The children were crowding around me—I had called them all together to tell them something. But little resolute Virginia just kept marching away pulling the red wagon. I asked her older brother to go get her, because she didn't seem to understand.

To my surprise, he called out, "Come on, Virginia, want some chewing gum?"

Virginia did not respond. Maybe she had been fooled a little too often at home.

That was a rather strange sight—men, women and children just sitting on the porch of the schoolhouse around the open door —sitting there from early morning till after dark, on a Saturday. An onlooker might well have asked the question little Edna finally asked when she had been there with her aunt for several hours. "What are you all doing here, just sitting?"

It would have been hard to explain to a little girl. It was not at all a child's affair, but the children had been brought along to take part in it as in everything else that went on in the community.

I was having trouble with the County School Board. The chairman of the Board had given me permission to use the vacant school room for the nursery school before he realized that I was connected with the Highlander Folk School. When this was discovered, I was asked to move. This School Board had a long record of opposition to all progressive movements down in our little community, and along with the coal company in Dyersville had always been hostile to the Folk School, objecting especially to its work of training trade union leaders and helping to organize workers into unions.

I prepared to move out after receiving the word from the Board, but one of the fathers happened to drop in as I was packing up the school equipment. No sooner had he heard the story than he dashed out to see some of the other parents. A committee of parents was immediately formed. They went to see the Board, they presented petitions formally at a Board meeting, they wrote letters and testimonials. But to no avail. In spite of their insistence that the nursery school was a blessing to the community and should be held in the school room, and that they had something to say about the use of the building on which they paid taxes, the Board continued to insist that I move.

The parents demanded that I stay. When the Board sent down a man to remove the stove from my room, they scurried around and found another one for me on the same day. Then word got around that the Board was sending a man to padlock me out. The parent committee hurried up to Dyersville to see a lawyer and found that such a procedure would be illegal. Hence this Saturday "sit-down" to await the Board at the door with this information.

Everybody was having a good time. It was good to be standing up for your rights, and good to be doing something different like this, almost a lark. The talk was militant and spirited.

"If we let the Board get away with this, we never will have any rights down here in Summerville!"

"There ain't goin' to be no padlock here on this door if I know anythin' about it!"

"Why, if they do that, we'll just all take our kids out of grammar school, that's what we'll do!"

The children played around on the steps within earshot of this talk (and also of the watchful admonitions that were constantly thrown out to them, which they did not heed, "Don't you run down there, you'll fall and skin your knees!")

I wonder what they made of it all.

P.S. The Board never came to put on the padlock. But the demands became so insistent that we moved out several weeks later, when we managed to secure another suitable place.

When I drove up, Julia was standing out by the big black washing pot crying wretchedly. I asked the big sister, who was getting ready to wash the clothes, what the trouble was. "Mother's goin' to comb her hair."

Sure enough, from the house came mother with a comb. Julia screamed and tried to run away, but her mother grabbed her and rather roughly combed her hair, while the child struggled and cried.

As soon as she was safe inside the car, she rumpled her hair all up again.

The child must have a tender scalp—or perhaps her hair becomes so frowzled that combing it (once a day?) is really a painful process.

Big sister Betty once told me that Julia was always a good girl, except when they wanted to comb her hair.

School-time conversation among three boys:
J.B.: "I got into the sugar and ate it, and I got whipped."
Wayne Edward: "I get whipped for cussin'."
Buddy: "Barbara gets whipped whenever she gets mean and tears things up."

Sunday afternoon, three o'clock, and the Hill's two-room shack (built after a fire at a cost of $25, nails and all) was absolutely spotless.

When I came in, Ella Caroline was asleep on the leather sofa, and Paul William in the baby's crib. The baby herself, now about two years old, was outside wandering around in the back yard. Through the open door I could see her climbing in and out of a rickety old outhouse.

My coming woke the two children. They beamed to see me, and Paul William immediately began to tell me a long tale about the new pony out in the barn; unfortunately I could understand very little of it, because of his defective speech. Ella Caroline, however, could only beam and beam silently as she put on her shoes and coat. "Say 'howdy' to your teacher!" Mrs. Hill prompted her.

Both children went out to play in the spacious lot behind the house; they were not sent out, but went eagerly of their own accord. I could see Paul William romping around with the pony, and Ella climbing on the rails of the hogpen.

The baby wandered in and out of the open door freely—her face and pretty blue snowsuit covered with the grime of play. Her mother apologized for her appearance, but wisely made no attempt to clean her up.

I went to take Susie her bag of fruit, because she had not come to school on the day of our Christmas party.

This family of five was temporarily located in a one-room log cabin that was in a very bad state of repair. Newspapers were stuffed around the edges of the one window to keep out the cold air, and a washboard was placed on the sill to cover the gap where a pane was out.

In spite of the fact that the room was very bare, reminding me much of the barn loft where I used to play an endless game of "poor family" with a little friend of mine, there was a lovely Christmas tree up on the bureau, all decked out in tinsel and shining things as a Christmas tree should be, and there were two new dolls under the tree.

Susie immediately began to gobble down one after another the apple, orange, raisins, and lollypop I had brought her—although she had stayed home from school because of indigestion.

"Give some to Laura," was her mother's prompt demand. Susie very willingly walked over to the bed where Laura was lying— the little girl's nose had been cut accidentally by an axe the day before—and gave her a good share of the fruit.

I had brought Susie some old Christmas cards to look at, too. One was a reproduction of a Madonna by Raphael. "I'd like to frame that and hang it on the wall," Mrs. Bennett said appreciatively, and placed it up out of Susie's reach.

Just then Mrs. Bennett's cousin dropped in, and the two women began to chat of this and that.

The ten-year-old boy of the family was carrying wood in while all this was going on, great chunks of wood that looked to me much too heavy for him to carry. After each chunk was in, he would stop and rest a minute and listen to the conversation.

"Go on out there and get the wood, it's getting dark," his mother kept nagging at him.

"His dad ought to give him a good licking once, and then you wouldn't have to keep talking to him so much," the cousin advised.

Just then Susie walked in front of my chair. Her mother yanked at her and slapped her face. "Don't you walk in front of Miss Lewis!"

Then she remembered the Madonna picture. She showed it to her cousin, and both women began to giggle softly.

"Did you see that?" Mrs. Bennett said to me, pointing to the naked boy baby.

"A nice thing to show your little girl!" the cousin laughed.

"I wonder why they put that on," Mrs. Bennett said, as she walked over to the bureau and put the picture out of sight.

Susie was playing on the floor with a little toy auto. I guess that it hit my shoe as she chugged around with it; I scarcely noticed. But her mother saw it and gave the child a whack, crossly demanding that she sit down in the corner. Susie couldn't seem to move; she just sat where she was, crying, whereupon her mother reached over to the window sill for the switch. At that Susie went promptly over to the corner.

I wished them a merry Christmas and went home along the lonely road through the woods.

Edna: "Ernestine, Jim (Ernestine's father) came down to our house last night, d-r-u-n-k! (this word drawled out to give emphasis). All he could say was 'Are you happy?' And his head kept shaking. Daddy asked him to sit down. He was so drunk he couldn't say anything but 'Are you happy?' Daddy took him home. He was drunk as a hound."

As she helped Julia into the car, sister Pauline yawned hugely.

"What's the matter, are you sleepy?" I asked.

"Yes, we was all up late last night. We was down to Trussel's tellin' jokes and riddles. Do you know about once there was two legs sittin' on one leg. No, two legs sittin' on three legs, and he had two legs—no, one leg . . . well, anyway, it's a man on a stool eatin' a bone. Ain't that funny! Mamma said that some night when we're down there she's goin' to play some tricks on us and scare us so we'll be afraid to come home."

Two new little children climbed into the car that day. I had made previous arrangements to stop for them. The mother's parting word to the older boy, as she helped the children into the car, was "Behave, Charles!" while their father called out to me from the gate, "Make them mind!" I gathered that perhaps these children did not "mind" any too well at home.

Here is a home that has not only six rooms but electric lights and a piano and radio. The oldest girl of the family, who goes to high school in Dyersville, is eighteen today, and there is to be a big party in the evening for community friends of all ages. This is not like the home I was in one day when one of the children suddenly turned to her mother and said, "Why this is May's birthday!" and that's all there was to it.

But even in this home there is no such thing as bedtime for the littlest one, the three-year-old girl. She is there at the party, watching the games, listening to the comic "readings" and songs. Even after she falls asleep no one puts her to bed for some time. She sleeps in the arms of adoring high school girls.

A little rumpus was going on among the crowd of children in the back seat of the car. Apparently someone was annoying Virginia. But her big brother, Wayne Edward, soon had it all straightened out. From my seat in front I heard:

Buddy to Wayne Edward: "Virginia's your sweetheart, 'cause you don't want anybody to do anything to her."

Teacher (intervening): "Why, Virginia's his little sister."

Wayne Edward to Buddy: "Yes, you think I want anybody to hurt my little sister? If it's just a baby playing with her and hurts her, that's all right, but not if anyone bigger hurts her."

Martin, five, and George, six, were going at each other fiercely out in the schoolyard. Some trouble over digging in the same hole. They were locked in a mad embrace, shovels in hand. I separated them, but before I knew it George had grabbed a near-by bucket and hurled it at Martin, whereupon Martin grabbed George's cap and ran off. I went inside with George, who was boiling mad. He frequently got into trouble with Martin, who was his next-door neighbor. Older boys in the neighborhood were apt to pick on him too. Amid a volley of curses I heard him spluttering, "I'd like to knock the guts out of Martin! My daddy *told* me to fight Martin, to throw anything I wanted to at him!"

Martin also was a child whom older boys in the public school tended to torment at recess time, when our group was out with theirs. "Mean old Martin!" they would call out in singsong, as though that were his regular nickname among neighborhood boys.

One day I was aghast to see Martin, in anger, pull out his pocket knife—every small boy has one, as important a part of his equipment as his overalls—and go right after the child who was teasing him.

No damage was done. Indeed, it may have been just a gesture— but it may have been more. It was Martin's own father who reported to us, with relish, one night when we picked him up in the car, the details of a fight that had just taken place on the street in Piedmont.

"Fate Thomas cut up Howard Johnson pretty bad with his knife. They was drunk, and Howard threw a bottle and hit him and he took out his knife and went at him. Fate never done nothin' like that before."

"Will the law do anything about it?" we asked.

"They'll try to but I don't think they will, because Howard is an overbearing man."

Conversation between two five-year-olds:

"Mac Scott stole our baby chickens."

"He stole ours too."

"Why don't you get out a warrant and put him in jail?"

When I left three-year-old Edward at his gate, I told his mother that he had had a fine sleep at school. It was the first day of our new all-day program, including a hot lunch and rest at school.

"Well well, that's fine," she said. "He ain't slept none in the daytime since last summer."

Mrs. Hill was quilting on the beautiful "Wedding Ring" quilt, which, stretched out on its frame, practically filled the walking space in the small room. But the four children were all there and began to show me the Christmas presents they had received from school and Sunday School and Santa Claus.

Mrs. Hill spoke up: "You don't know how Ella entertains us of an evening! She tells us every story she hears at nursery school, and she don't miss a word!"

Then, even though the child was present, "Does Ella ever give you any trouble at school?"

"Indeed, no!" I answered, and meant it. Ella Caroline was as sunny and cheerful and peaceful and cooperative a child as one could find anywhere.

"I just wondered," Mrs. Hill continued. "She's always good here at home too. She never does a thing she ain't supposed to."

Julia had a terrible abscess on her face; there was a lump on her cheek as big as an apple.

We drove her and her mother to the clinic at the hospital, but when we stopped the car at the door, Julia, with characteristic terror of doctors, began to cry and hold back, and refused to get out of the car. Beside herself, she took off her shoes and threw them on the floor of the car.

Her mother's way of trying to deal with this was to whisper persuasively, "Come on now, Julie, or the Booger will get you."

But so far as Julia was concerned, the Booger already had her. In this case, such a threat had no effect.

But listen to Ella Caroline, five, talking to another child: "I wouldn't steal, would you? The old Boogerman will get you."

Soon after we arrived at school, Edward ran up to me saying happily, "Miss Lewis, I've got me a baby at home!"

Hardly ever before had Edward come running up to me to tell me anything. He was one of our shyest, most untalkative, solemn-faced children.

But today he actually seemed elated, livelier and happier than I had ever seen him. I could hardly believe it when I heard him humming as he stood beside me, waiting for the rope I was tying for him.

When I took the children home, I went into the house with him to see the baby, the eighth child come to inhabit this two-room cabin. Edward ran right up to the bed where his mother lay with the baby. She drew him close to her with one arm, giving him a few affectionate pats while she uncovered the baby with the other, so that we could see him.

"Edward's crazy over him," she said, "only he'd like to have him big enough to get right down on the floor and play with him!"

Mealtime conversation at the nursery school:

Annie Pearl: "Dr. Brown gave us our baby. Bud and Margaret and me went to sister's and when we come back the baby was there."
Wayne Edward: "Dr. Thomas brought me."
J.B.: "God brought you."
Wayne Edward: "He made us."

That's all. They go on eating.

Wayne Edward came galloping up to me in the nursery school play yard on his "horse." He brought it to a sudden stop, rearing it up to a precarious height. "Are you gonna vote for me?" he yelled, and without waiting for an answer he was off, galloping toward a group of children across the yard. Reining in his horse there, he shouted to them also: "Gonna vote for me?" And off he pranced toward another group, where the queer little performance was repeated.

County elections were just over, and there was no telling what

Wayne Edward had seen and heard and soaked in around home.

Buddy knew about the elections too. "Jim Edwards used to be sheriff but he ain't now," he announced to me on that same day.

Everyone was concerned over the loss of the elections, "loss" meaning that Jim Edwards had been the people's man, as opposed to the coal company's man who was now in office. Two years ago the people, meaning the miners, ex-miners, relief workers of the county, had been strong enough to elect many of their own representatives—men who were friendly to labor regardless of party —with the help of "Labor's Political Conference," their own organization.

Now, however, things had not gone so well. The Conference was no longer active, the poll tax was of course no help, and there may have been other factors. I happened to come into the possession of a letter written by one of the Summerville men at the time, indicating his view of the political situation. I can't vouch for the authenticity of the "facts" he quotes. Indeed, I have no way of knowing that these things actually happened in the way and for the reasons stated here. But this is one man's opinion, and strong feeling. Perhaps it is interesting enough to quote in part at this point, since this is J.B.'s father speaking:

"A little Ring of two-bit nit-wit politicians went around in the coves and hills and back woods and geathered up a lot of the most ignorant bunch of W.P.A. workers that never reads a newspaper never owned a radio that doesn't know right from wrong and hauled them in to the Democratic County Convention at Dyersville to vote for a chairman that the Coal Co. was backing. I would say 9/10 of the people today could not tell you what it was all about. . . . I aske several of the people at Dyersville that day what the meeting was about. No one knew and no one since can tell you what it was all about, they won't talk for they are in fear of loosing their only means of livelyhood, a mere starvation wage."

We were parked in front of Edward's house, waiting for him. His mother was hurriedly getting him ready for school, washed and cleanly dressed, a process which never took place until the car actually arrived. The door of the house had been left open and we could easily see Edward inside, having his clothes changed.

"I wouldn't get dressed where everybody can see me," Buddy spoke up. "I know where my daddy goes whenever he has to get dressed and there's somebody there. He goes into his room. My daddy sleeps in his underwear and shirt and socks."

Ina Lee's grandmother rode into town with us on our regular five o'clock trip for the evening mail. On these trips she never failed to speak of the "purty lights" in the town, meaning the neon signs over the cafes.

"I'm goin' to bring Ina Lee with me tomorry night, so she can see all these purty lights. Pore little thing, she don't git no chance to go nowheres or see nothin'. She cried to come with me this evenin', but I told her if hit warn't rainin' or snowin' tomorry she could come. Hit'd be something new for her."

I found Mrs. Johnson in the midst of her mopping on that winter day when I called to find out why Barbara, now three and a half, was staying home from nursery school. I urged Mrs. Johnson not to stop her work on my account, I would only stay a minute; but she insisted on drawing up two chairs by the stove and sitting down with me.

Barbara, who was there in the room with us, decided that she'd continue the mopping if her mother wouldn't. With a thump and a slosh she soon had the big dripping mop, along with half the contents of the bucket, on the floor.

"Barbara honey, *don't* do that," her mother exclaimed. "That's too hard for you."

Barbara sloshed away determinedly, paying not the least attention to her mother.

"*Don't*, Barbara, do you hear?"

Another slosh, with water spilling all over the floor.

At this Mrs. Johnson got up and I fully expected to see her take the mop away from Barbara. But she stooped and wrung it out and let the child go on, even as she continued to prod her with "Don't" and "You mustn't do this."

In fact, each time that Barbara swung the saturated mop onto the floor, Mrs. Johnson sprang up and wrung it out for her, saying at the same time, "Stop this now, Barbara, do you hear?"

"Barbara used to mind so well," Mrs. Johnson explained to me, "but now she don't seem to want to. I don't know what's got into her."

Martin was another child who had been staying home from nursery school recently. I knew that he had just had the mumps, but thought he must surely be ready to return to school by now.

When I stopped to see his mother, she explained that she was keeping him home until his little brother Marvin caught the mumps and got over them too.

"Marvin would raise such a squawl if I let Martin go off without him. He would want to go so badly too, and couldn't understand why he would have to stay home."

As I walked off down the road I wondered if she was keeping him home because she really couldn't bear to hear the least one squawling unhappily, or if it actually never occurred to her that it might be a good idea to try to help him understand why things couldn't always go his way.

The Clark family was having a hard time. After Mrs. Clark had died, a few months ago, the father took his family of six children to live with his sister. This sister already had a daughter of eighteen and the daughter's baby to look out for, and the house had only two rooms.

Things did not go well. I heard that Mr. Clark had a bitter hatred for his sister's child, who was illegitimate.

One night he just bundled up his little family and trudged down the mountain with them, to stay with some other kinfolk.

But before long they were back in our neighborhood, established by themselves in a little house that looked something like a garage from the outside. I went over one December day to see how they were getting along. The two youngest children had been coming to my nursery school. There was Doris, a small, thin child of eleven who had been promoted to the position of mother of the family, standing by the kitchen stove stirring the kraut in the frying pan. Potatoes were boiling in a big kettle, and a pot of coffee stood on the back of the stove.

"Are you cooking the supper, Doris?"

"No'm. Bill put it on and I'm watchin' it." (Bill was the oldest boy, sixteen.)

Edna, five, was standing in a corner by the stove looking at her sister's reading book. She was barefoot, in spite of the cold, and the dress her aunt had made her had lost its buttons and was anything but clean. Vera, six, was washing out some socks in an old lard pail. Little four-year-old Mac was playing around outside, and daddy was off at his W.P.A. work.

I asked Edna to show me through their house, as I had never been in it before. We all wandered through the almost bare three rooms, and discovered Bill in the adjoining woodshed, "stealing" nuts out of a bag.

"Oh, Bill, daddy will whip you!"

But Bill only smiled and passed the nuts around to all the children, offering me some too.

Doris kept a very careful eye on the young ones, eager to show me that she knew her manners, and how to run a house.

"Hang up your clothes, Vera!"

"Don't get your feet on the bed!"

"Mac, you mustn't leave soap lying on the bed!"

Edna pointed proudly to her Christmas doll, hung on a nail high on the wall to keep it safe, as is the common custom here.

Mac, sparkling-eyed, sturdy, clothed in a dirty suit much too big for him, his feet stuffed into girl's slippers, began to show me how he could jump onto the floor from an old trunk. The brother and sisters watched him encouragingly and adoringly, and the two older ones looked at me with private appreciative smiles, as parents would, when he burst into one of his bright grins.

As I left, Doris, child that she was, spoke the cordial words expected of any housewife: "What's your hurry? Won't you take dinner with us? Come back!"

So the Summerville child grows out of babyhood, and becomes even more firmly entrenched in the life of the community. Scarcely any of his parents' activities go on without his little face somewhere in the picture, taking in the whole thing. Indeed, he doesn't actually follow his father to his job, but during the lay-off periods when his dad is home, he hardly leaves his side.

Life for him is still in many ways very much the stronghold of delight and comfort that it was when he was a small baby. True, now he has given up cuddling and kissing and hugging, to a great extent, because he has become a big boy and cuddling is just for babies. He takes that for granted; it's the way of the whole community. But still he feels the strong support of mother's and father's love. Still he has older sisters and brothers to turn to for additional care.

And still many of the frustrations common to other children in other places are unknown to him. He stays up as late as he pleases, and even gets to sleep with his beloved daddy, in many cases. No one cares if he grabs up food at any time of day when he is hungry, and if he's sick but doesn't want to stay in bed, he isn't made to. A daily bath is an unheard-of thing, and even a rigorous routine of hand and face washing several times a day is not insisted on. Of course, he gets washed before he goes to nursery school or Sunday School, but not necessarily before breakfast. He is expected to be present when guests come and to join in the conversation if he wants to, though not to hold the center of attention.

Indeed, he is very close to the whole business of his parents' living. He calls the man next door "Jim" just as his parents do. He knows about drunkenness, about the violence that crops up sometimes; he knows about death and funerals; he sees his parents get "converted" at the revival; he takes part in the work of the household, and in the family's recreation. When a new baby arrives, he is likely to accept it with less shock and jealousy than would be the case if he were an only child and one living in a family where differentiation between the status and privileges of members of the household is considerably greater than it is in a Summerville family.

Perhaps the one and only thing that parents attempt to shield carefully from him is the sexual relationship. He does not really know where babies come from. But he thinks he knows: it is as natural for him to believe that the doctor brings them as to believe that Santa Claus brings toys at Christmas and that Jesus can burn up the world. So we are led to assume that this is no problem to him, at least at this early age.

By the time he is six he has absorbed a good deal of the traditional attitude toward what is right and wrong, good and bad. He has a vague concept of a powerful Jesus up there in the sky somewhere. He learns early that he should look down on colored people—though Negroes never settled on the mountain and there are very few of them ever to be seen. He must mind his manners in the presence of visitors, and sometimes he even learns a few rudiments of "table manners," though these can scarcely be very exacting in homes where the supply and variety of cutlery and dishes are somewhat limited, and eating does not always mean actually sitting down in chairs at a table three times a day.

He is taught that stealing is wrong; however, in a community where petty thievery is very common, even in some of the "best" families, where perhaps it becomes associated with the independent urge to get what is your due, this early training may have little effect.

While there is some possibility that he may occasionally see the naked bodies of all members of his own family, he takes over from his parents the idea that only shame is to be associated with such things, in public.

And as he goes about with his parents and hears them talk, he is undoubtedly learning to copy not only their cordial and hospitable ways, but also the militant and independent spirit they show at times, when their rights and privileges are at stake.

And the fighting and feuding tradition of his people, though it is certainly more a thing of the past than of the present, is not unknown to him. Freely discussed in his presence are the shootings that go on occasionally in the honky-tonks, the street fight in Piedmont. He knows how one-armed Hiram Adams lost that arm—as a result of a gun shot. Indeed, his father encourages him, not to pick fights, but to fight as viciously as needs be to uphold his own rights and protect himself—and by all means to protect his little sister on all occasions. Yet certainly one does not think of these children as a fighting breed. Many parents report that their children go through the day at home as peaceably and happily on the whole as they do at the nursery school. This life of theirs appears to be one that does not engender many of the conflicts common to early childhood elsewhere.

That it is a completely easygoing Utopia from the children's point of view, entirely free of all frustrations and troubles, is of course not the case. As we have seen, children are led to expect physical punishment for disobedience, particularly if it involves what is considered serious disrespect toward elders.

Such punishment and pressures have varying effects on various children, as is to be expected. There are children like Paul William who are far from docile, who rebel and defy and go their own way. Others are more readily intimidated, or accept more easily the parental dictates. And indeed the discipline itself is applied with varying degrees of firmness. Always it is clear-cut in its intentions, but actually in the majority of cases turns out to be somewhat unskillfully administered. Many children can easily "get away" with a good deal in comparatively small matters, because their indulgent parents do not know how to be sufficiently consistent and firm. They fail to follow up their commands with action. But on the other hand there are a few harsh parents who unreasonably slap and yank their children around as their moods direct.

In spite of variations, however, we can trace a general thread running through the Summerville pattern of discipline. We can say that by and large Summerville children are not often actually physically mistreated. Many are never whipped, and those who are, find it only an occasional experience. Verbal scolding and threats of whippings and the Boogerman are applied much more frequently than actual physical pressure.

This is not to imply that discipline is so "lax" as to permit a child to do such a serious thing as kick his grandmother and escape without a whipping. However, it is very difficult to picture a Summerville child in the act of attacking his grandmother. The community's code of behavior surrounds such acts with a strong taboo, and the children early learn what this code of behavior is. Regardless of what their parents *say*, the children take over what they see them *do*. The part of the code that is seriously and deeply meaningful to the parents—such as respect for elders, for religion, and for the forms of hospitality—becomes meaningful for the children, too, and probably has a much more powerful effect on them than the discipline rather feebly enforced by threats of the hickory stick.

The picture of Summerville children begins to take shape as one of children who, indeed, probably do "fear" to show an uninhibited and violent type of defiance toward their elders, due more to the attitude of parental taboo that surrounds them than to the actual discipline to which they are subjected.

Though a few children at one end of the scale may really be intimidated by rough parents, and some at the other extreme may entirely rule the roost, by and large the demand for obedience turns out to be something that the majority of children seem able to accept in their stride, perhaps not without momentary defiance but apparently without a deep-seated antagonism and resentment. Perhaps this is because they feel secure in the love of those who administer the discipline. Perhaps it is because this discipline involves so little pressure to give up their fundamental pleasures and remold their ways. It is not something that "unreasonably" (as they might feel) restrains them from their urges every moment of their lives. There is scarcely need for such restriction even from the point of view of the parent in Summerville where children, whether or not to their ultimate advantage, for the most part do not find themselves in constant conflict with adults and with the routine of living that is expected of them.

Moreover, the little Summerville girl or boy, with his big yard and barn lot and adjoining woods to play in, unsupervised, has a whole world of his own where he is free to do as he likes. This outdoor life helps to give him a certain sturdiness to compensate for what is at the same time working against him. He still may not get enough sleep. He still eats irregularly and improperly; he plays around outdoors when he should be "sick in bed"; he is "doctored" at times only by Superstition, and is exposed not only to serious burning but to a great array of other accidents that are bound to occur when he handles axes and pitchforks and goes around barefoot six months out of the year.

This world of his, though it may be "his own," remains a rather limited one, physically bounded chiefly by his own familiar home and lot, with only an occasional journey into the larger yet similar world of Piedmont or Dyersville. And only now and then does an outlander intrude his strange accent into the scene.

THE SCHOOL YEARS

❀❀❀❀❀❀❀❀❀❀❀❀❀❀❀❀❀❀❀❀❀❀❀❀

THE SCHOOLHOUSE, which now becomes a large factor in the lives of most Summerville children of school age, whether or not consistently each year, is a low, many-windowed frame building of two rooms. We can see at a glance that it is very superior to most of the other small rural schoolhouses scattered throughout the county. True, it does not have modern plumbing, but it is a spacious, well-kept building, lighted by electricity. The explanation of its superiority lies in the fact that it was donated to the county by the public-spirited and greatly loved Dr. Lillian Johnson, who worked among the Summerville people as teacher, friend, adviser, before the days of the Highlander Folk School. Indeed, she lived and worked and brought the community together in the building that now houses the Folk School.

Not only do we see that the schoolhouse is a superior building, but when we step inside the big room we see that unusual things have been going on here. There are shelves and shelves of excellent library books. There are braided rugs on exhibit, and tables set aside to display handmade baskets and metal and wood work. But we notice that these finished products are on exhibit, and a little dusty at that. There are no traces of any such things now actually in the making.

For ten years—up until 1938—the Summerville children were fortunate to have an unusually gifted, ingenious, understanding teacher (known to the outside world as a distinguished writer of children's books)—Miss May Justus, herself a mountaineer, who knew how to make school really meaningful to children. With her help these boys and girls, to whom she was more of a mother than a teacher, learned how to take the odds and ends they found around them and make something useful and beautiful out of them. They made baskets from pine needles and honeysuckle vines; they transformed flour sacks into curtains, and out of tin they learned to make candlesticks, flower holders, and book ends. And they had the satisfaction of earning money for their books and for the daily soup pot from the sale of their handwork in Nashville, Boston, New York, and Washington, D.C.

Of her school, Miss Justus told me: "We used to have five different kinds of work going on at once, not just one lesson after another. In fact, I always had more for the children to do than they could possibly do. That's why their desks weren't all carved up, and why I never had any trouble making them behave in the schoolroom."

But at the present time, the desks are all carved up and spitballs sometimes fly. The inexperienced young teacher, eager to do the job well and maintain "proper discipline," keeps on hand a goodly supply of hickory switches, which do not lie idle by any means. School has again become chiefly a matter of the conventional 3 R's —and of theoretically quiet waiting for your turn to recite. Sometimes it can be a long wait, with thirty-five or forty children to be helped through the eight grades all by one teacher in one room—indeed a task to floor the best-intentioned.

The teacher has tried to remedy the situation as best she knew. One year she arranged the day so that the younger children came to school in the morning and the older ones in the afternoon. But the parents objected to this finally, so she resorted, wisely, to allowing the little ones to spend a good deal of their time outdoors playing in the sun when the weather permitted, with sometimes an older child along to read to them or teach them games.

For these younger ones, then, the school day, even under the present regime, does not actually turn out to be always a long, quiet, sedentary one, and thus is undoubtedly not nearly so "frustrating" as the conventional school is commonly supposed to be —though this is not to imply, of course, that it does not retain many of the disadvantages of the "old-fashioned" conventional country school.

In considering what "school" means to the Summerville six-to-twelve-year-olds, then, it is important to understand the nature of the two "regimes," both of which have affected the lives of the majority of this generation of school children: the present regime operating on conventional lines, though still retaining a good deal of informality and comparative freedom for the younger children for at least part of the time; the other a regime whose days were crowded with constructive activity and ringed round with games and picnics, stories, songs, clubs, and fun. This was a genuinely progressive school in those days, such as one would never expect to find on a mountain top in the backwoods country. In fact, the opportunities it offered, particularly in the areas of literature and handicrafts, were extraordinary by any measuring rod.

It is also important to keep in mind that in a rural community like Summerville, twelve or thirteen is not the usual age of completion of the eighth grade. The few stragglers and strugglers who have reached the heights of the upper grades are apt to be fully grown adolescents of fifteen, sixteen. What we have said of the "school years" hardly applies to them in all respects. For them, school is another story and belongs in the next chapter.

The Highlander Folk School was under attack. Not that there was any shooting going on, but an employee of the Coal Company had launched a vigorous campaign to get the school to move off the mountain with its "dangerous" ideas of unionism.

The people in Summerville, however, had a long history of unionism behind them—their fathers and grandfathers had joined the United Mine Workers of America as far back as 1898, long before the days of the Folk School—and they were in entire sympathy with the work of the school.

Members of the Highlander staff as well as members of the community circulated petitions in order to have tangible proof of public support.

I stopped in at Campbells' one day with one of these petitions which they had not yet signed. Mrs. Campbell was nursing the new baby. The two little children, two and four years old, were racing around barefoot through the two rooms, playing with the new wagon which was one of the fruits of Mr. Campbell's new job over in Hillsboro where a military camp was going up.

The oldest child, Mary Ella, about 11, was ironing one of her dresses on the bed. She was getting ready to go off and spend the night with her grandmother in town. "That's no place to iron!" her mother reproved her good-naturedly. But poised little Mary Ella was not to be stopped by the presence of an outsider. With her gay laugh she just said, "Oh well, I can't manage it so well any other place," and finished her ironing in her own way.

I talked to Mrs. Campbell about the petition. She said she would be glad to sign it and thought her husband would be too, when he came home. "Yes," broke in Mary Ella who was listening to the conversation, "he'll sign it if he thinks it won't get him mixed up in no harm!"

When I actually handed the petition to Mrs. Campbell, along with the pencil, it was Mary Ella who stepped up and signed her mother's name. "I can't read or write," Mrs. Campbell explained, much to my surprise. She was a young woman, and I had not encountered illiteracy in Summerville before, except in the cases of a few very old people.

Mary Ella offered me an apple from the tow sack in the corner, bundled up her dress and other necessary articles, and we drove off to town.

From the nursery school car we could see J.B.'s two older brothers, seven and nine, wandering slowly along the railroad track. This was a day when they were not having school. "Yeah, they're pickin' up scrap iron," little J.B. explained. "You can sell scrap iron for money."

When I stopped in at Browns' to see about getting some coal from the small mine where one of the sons worked, I found nine-year-old Louise at home there with her mother, even though it was a school day. "She's taken a notion she don't want to go no more," Mrs. Brown explained, "and I hate to force her. She's got plenty of time yet. She liked it till she fell out with Mary Ann one day, and after that she just didn't go no more."

I took Adam, nine, with me over to the clinic to have the doctor look at his sore throat. His mother said his temperature had gone "way yonder," and she thought he had tonsilitis. As she was busy washing that day and could not come along, I got the doctor's instructions for her. "Tell her to keep him in bed even if she has to do it with a board!" the doctor said, evidently well aware of how difficult a feat it was to make these mountain children stay in bed.

But I learned afterward that Adam had not gone to bed nor even stayed home. "He won't miss school," his mother said. "I know there was two or three days when he oughtn't to have gone, but he wouldn't stay at home. He was so hoarse he could hardly talk, and Miss Johnson had to read his lesson for him, and I'd say, 'Son, you better stay home,' but he'd say, 'I *won't* stay home,' and there was just nothin' you could do."

The Duncan girls—five of them, ranging from seven to nineteen—were usually among the first to arrive for the regular Sunday afternoon Harp Sing at the Folk School. This Sing started out as a session for adults, but was soon crowded also with the children who came along as a matter of course.

And look at these little girls, the seven- and nine- and twelve-year-olds with lipstick and nail polish just like their big sisters.

There they sit, studying the songbooks and singing away as seriously and wholeheartedly as their parents.

Nor are lipstick and paint and powder and Harp Singing the only evidences that the little girls of Summerville are partaking in adult life to as full extent as they can.

At recess time over at the public school, tobacco pouches are in evidence among some of the girls as well as the boys—not flaunted openly, but pulled out more or less in secret.

Yet nine-year-old Louise did walk along the tracks one day, quite frankly smoking what certainly appeared to be a cigarette.

That Saturday morning we picked up two ten-year-old boys who were walking the two miles into town, one to get groceries at the store for his mother, and the other entrusted with money to pay off something on the bill.

An expert on child rearing from the State Parent-Teacher Association was holding a series of lectures at the public school building in Piedmont. We took a carload of mothers in for one meeting, having very little idea of the nature of the lectures.

It was a mistake. The lecturer was addressing a different kind of audience. I think she must have had in mind the wealthy families who spent their summers on the grounds of the resort in Piedmont. The suggestions she had for "little ways to help your children learn responsibility" must have fallen upon amused ears, at least among our group of parents.

"Why, May (eight years old) helps me almost as much as a grown woman!" Mrs. Henderson said, almost indignantly, on the ride home.

There were guests from Birmingham at the Highlander Folk School—a family including a little boy and girl of about six and eight. These children were lively and loved to talk, and were pretty well aware of their cleverness, too.

A neighbor who had been with us one day at dinner expressed disapproval to me afterwards of the way this little boy and girl had behaved at the table, talking so much and "getting attention."

It wasn't long afterward that this same neighbor's own little girl, nine, had occasion to eat dinner with us. She sat there, head down, eating away without a word, and seemed surprised and flustered when we talked to her, and scarcely knew how to answer, though indeed she was not at all one of the extremely shy and inarticulate children of the community.

During recess a little girl about twelve came around to our side of the schoolhouse to play with the children for a moment. (At this time the nursery school was located in the public school building.)

She went over to the see-saw where Ernestine was sitting alone, waiting for someone to get on the other end with her. "Will you get on, Wayne Edward?" Ernestine called. "No thanks," was the answer, since Wayne Edward was busy at something else. The little visitor then commented to him, "I didn't think you'd want to get on with a little *girl*."

Nine-year-old Caroline Smith volunteered to help me one week during the summer when my N.Y.A. girl was laid off. Caroline could not, of course, assume full responsibility with the children, but she gave invaluable help when it came to drawing that pail of water that was needed in a hurry, or washing up the cups.

Caroline was not at all one of the "Yes'm" children. She had a good deal to say—of course, she was fairly used to me—and on those afternoons when we cleaned up the school together she poured out torrents of talk, thoroughly enjoying it too, especially the gruesome and "scary" aspects of what she had to say. She dwelt particularly on the burning of her sister's baby. "She looks like a corpse, all the hide burned off her side, and she's got the least little arms and legs. I think I'd die if anything was to happen to her . . . You know, I've seen lots of dead people. My grandmother died in the bed while we was eating."

And on another afternoon she was full of tales of the "ball of fire" they had seen over at their house the night before when a bunch of the neighbors had been passing the time together. "That means someone's going to die, sure. Over at Turners' they seen one once and someone *did* die."

This led to the recital of other tales of horrors and apparitions and fearsome sights that had been topics of conversation the night before. Apparently this was one of the ways of finding excitement in Summerville of an evening. "There was a queer ball dipping up and down in the sky . . . and my brother seen two people in white walking up the railroad track ahead of him but the nearer he'd get the farther away they'd get, and he never could catch up to them . . . then we made a rag man and put it out at the gate to scare Ethel, and she yelled! Like Mac used to put rag men on the tracks and make the trains stop."

When Margaret, ten, helped her little sister into the car I asked why she hadn't gone to school today. "Mother's washing and I have to help her with it."

After school hours and during the summer Ralph, eight, glued himself to his big seventeen-year-old brother, Paul, and the two were practically always seen together.

If we heard a shot in the woods back of the nursery school, we could be pretty sure that it was Paul out hunting rabbits, and that soon we would see him walk by on the path at the side of the house, Ralph trotting along behind him and the dog trotting along behind Ralph.

Junior had been in nursery school the year before and had started to attend the grammar school that fall. But lately I noticed that he was always at home when I drove around to get his little sister.

"Why don't you go to school any more, Junior?" I would ask.

"Oh, I don't want to," was the only answer I could ever get.

Slightly deaf and very timid, he must have found school difficult, and no one at home felt it necessary to force him to go.

I talked with his teacher about him one day and found that she considered him "sexually unbalanced." She had found him masturbating in school once, though she didn't think he realized he was doing it. "I never was so shocked. I've never had a child do that before."

The two Hill children had dropped out of school, too—Paul William who was six and had just started, and Mary Ann who was ten. I never did hear the whole story, but it boiled down to the fact that Mary Ann had had some trouble with one of her class-mates, Wilsie, and the teacher had taken Wilsie's part. There ensued a scene in which Wilsie called Mary Ann's mother a liar, whereupon Mrs. Hill slapped her down good and hard and took the children out of school.

When I asked Paul William one day why he wasn't going to school, he simply said "I don't know."

There were two little girls in the community who had been promoted to position of mother of the family because of the deaths of their own mothers. Neither of them went to school.

Bessie Norwood, sister of our little Billy, was only eight or possibly nine; indeed she didn't have any idea of her age, and I could only guess at it. Though she did not do the cooking, she was left at home to take care of the house and watch out for Billy when he came home from nursery school. I noticed that she even took it upon herself to "train" him to a certain extent. She was riding with us as far as the crossing one day when the little boy began to laugh and call out in derision at the one-legged man who was walking down the road.

"Don't you laugh at him!" she said seriously. "He couldn't help it if his leg got cut off. Daddy'll whip you when we get home!"

The other little girl who was trying to be a mother was Doris, whom we have already seen in her home. She brought all of the younger children to the schoolhouse on the day the county health officer came to inoculate. The crying four-year-old she carried in her arms, though he was much too heavy a load for her.

After it was over, she stopped with the children out by the swing in the schoolyard, and engineered turns for all of them, but I noticed that she never took a turn herself. It probably never occurred to her to do so, even though she was just a little girl herself and certainly not too old for swinging.

It is 10:30 on the Friday before Christmas. The schoolroom is beautiful with holly, tinsel, Christmas bells, and a magnificent

Christmas tree. The children are dressed up in their very best Sunday suits and dresses, because this is one of the biggest occasions in the year. Their mothers and some of their fathers and younger brothers and sisters have come to hear them recite their Christmas "pieces" and sing the well-known Christmas songs.

The recitations appear to be agonizing experiences to many of the children. Adam stands there on the platform awkward in his unaccustomed coat and pants, racing and mumbling and stumbling through the memorized words in a low voice that is scarcely audible. His arms are frozen to his sides except for the dreaded moments when he must try to move them in the fixed gestures the teacher has taught him to use as appropriate accompaniment for the piece.

But after the agony comes applause, and the warm and appreciative smiles from his parents. And best of all, at the end of the program, the present from the teacher—no mere five-cent trinket, but a really generous gift.

The hot summer sun doesn't deter these youngsters. The nine or ten of them who have come over to the Folk School this afternoon (this is Wednesday afternoon, belonging to the six-to-twelves of the neighborhood) are out in the ball field having a game of baseball, with a Highlander staff member in charge. If these threatening clouds really result in a downpour, the children will go inside and model with the clay they dug last week, or paint pictures on big sheets of paper.

Maybe next week they'll all go for a "swim" (unfortunately, there is not much more than a muddy wading hole available) or will just watch the well-digging machine that bores away out in the orchard with such a noisy, monotonous yet fascinating persistency.

I was over at Wilsie's house, sitting in the porch swing, enjoying the shade and visiting with her mother. We had just completed a round in the flower garden where Mrs. Ladd had picked me a bunch of the flowers I had admired most, nameless so far as we both knew, but adequately described by Mrs. Ladd as "them flowers that stoop down."

Wilsie, nine, was playing with a schoolmate of about the same age at one end of the spacious porch. They were carrying on a very lively kind of "play." Wilsie had something she called a "typewriter" which she had cleverly constructed out of a corn-flakes box. (*What* are these children doing with a typewriter? I wondered.) I caught bits of conversation about "W.P.A. office . . . go up to Dyersville and get your work card . . . now you have to wait."

Yes, they were enacting this whole business, such a familiar one to their fathers.

I asked Wilsie later how she got the idea for this play. "Oh, I just heard dad and mother talking so much about it."

Edna, at nursery school, reporting on her next door neighbor: "Did you know Wilsie got a whipping yesterday? 'Cause she said she wished her sister would die."

The Parent-Teacher Association was giving another play for the benefit of the new hot-lunch program. Mr. and Mrs. Smith were both in the play, so on the night of the performance the year-old baby of the family was entrusted to the oldest son, aged twelve.

I marveled at his skill in nursemaiding! Sitting right behind him I could not help but notice the complete ease and mastery with which he tried out one little adult trick after another to quiet the baby when it began to whimper—little clucking sounds, jiggling it in his lap, diverting it with some gadget or other.

He seemed to be as much at home with a baby on his lap, there in that crowded audience, as he undoubtedly would be out on his front steps sittin' a-whittlin'.

Mr. Priest was an ingenious man. I never knew what to expect to find when I went over to that cabin. There was a period when he was trying his hand at woodcarving, and another time when he was making glass cigarette trays out of old bottles. He even told me once that he was writing a book, all about the wretched life of poor folks like the Summerville people, how they are shoved around at election time and are powerless to do anything about it—but the day will come when the silence they keep will end!

One day when I went to call on the family, I found Mr. Priest at home taking care of the two younger children. His wife had gone off to stay with her grandmother in town for a few days. He was sitting there in the middle of the dark, disordered cabin, reading *Grapes of Wrath,* from the Folk School library.

I wondered if a man like Jim Priest looked upon child rearing and parenthood with eyes that differed from his neighbors' in any important respects.

"What do you want your children to be when they grow up?" I asked him once. He was stumped and had no answer. "Well, I guess that's something I just never thought about," he said, finally. His oldest boy was ten.

Summerville children of ten seem to be, in some ways, small adults. They are still ever-present in the picture of family and community life, and the responsibilities they are able to assume have increased considerably. Mary Ella not only writes for her mother, but knows her dad's ways with an insight that is probably almost as keen as her mother's. May helps "almost as much as a grown woman."

This added responsibility does not mean, however, that life has become a burden for the school-age child, and that there is no time to play. To judge from the amount of leisurely sitting and swinging on porches that can be observed at almost any time of day in Summerville, household tasks around the average small cabin are not sufficiently demanding to keep the mother busy all day, to say nothing of the daughter or son. There is still time— and space—for free roaming about and following one's own inclinations.

Yes, in spite of the fact that school is now something to reckon with. As we have seen, the matter of schooling (like that of other ambitions for children), seems to be taken very lightly by the majority of parents, few of whom managed to finish the eighth grade themselves. The Summerville picture is not the one that might be conjured up of every child of six and over being rigidly shoved off to school every day against his will. (This does not mean, of course, that there are not some parents who do insist on school attendance for their children and sacrifice generously to make it possible, even looking forward hopefully to sending the children to high school some day.)

Furthermore, there is every reason to believe that, whether we refer to the old regime or the new, school is hardly in every way the frustrating bugaboo it is often considered to be, even for those who are made to attend regularly. In fact, it provides one of the few occasions for social get-together that are possible in a community of this sort.

Then, too, it is likely that the small one-room school does not present such a strenuous situation of competition as may exist in larger "conventional" city schools. The Summerville child just entering the first grade, for instance, does not find himself suddenly obliged to enter into competition with the thirty-five other children who are in the room. Of these thirty-five, in his own small group there are only seven or eight against whom he must begin to measure himself. Yet he has the satisfaction of being there, in the same room, the same inner sanctum, where sit the biggest and toughest boys in the neighborhood.

At the same time, one might ask, does he perhaps feel the necessity to compete in some ways even with these big children, just because he is there in the same situation with them, even though the teacher expects no academic competition? Possibly the answer is, No more so than he does at home. After all, many of the big "tough" boys are the brothers of the younger children, and all are more or less known to each other already. This schoolroom is not so different from a Summerville home situation. As older children help care for the little ones at home, so they continue to look out for them at school. Competition may be in the air to a certain extent, but there is also cooperation. This does not mean, of course, that the present school situation, in contrast to the "old regime," provides everything to be desired. Its faults are not so much in what it offers as in what it fails to offer in the way of stimulation to the developing intelligence and personality, and an understanding handling of individual children's difficulties.

But because of his contact with Miss Justus, and to some extent with the Highlander Folk School, we may be sure that our school-age child has been exposed to some really progressive teaching, including a number of the so-called "creative" materials and opportunities that he might not have met up with if he had stayed close to his home and yard. There is hardly a school child in Summerville who has not at some time held a piece of potter's clay in his hands and molded it to suit himself. For a number of children there have been piano lessons, for most children the chance to paint and draw, to hammer and saw and weave and sew. To what extent these opportunities have changed the direction of their growth it would be impossible to say at the present time.

To all outward appearances, life for our six-to-twelve-year-olds flows on much as it always has for them, in what seems to be the same easygoing tenor, in spite of the fact that they now go to school and carry added responsibilities in their homes. They are still children in status, especially when it comes to the question of theoretical obedience to elders, and they by no means escape the hickory switch or the threat of it either at home or at school, because of the inches that have added themselves to their statures.

They are still children who are keenly aware that there are certain things that are "proper" to do and others that would be shockingly indecent and out of place, things that simply "are not done."

They are still children—growing children—who are not made to eat or sleep or take care of themselves as they should.

And last, they are still children who know no world but Summerville. It is still large enough, and small enough, for them and they appear to be happy there and at ease.

ADOLESCENCE

✿✿✿✿✿✿✿✿✿✿✿✿✿✿✿✿✿✿✿✿✿✿✿

I WAS TALKING with one of the N.Y.A. girls who helped me at the nursery school. She was eighteen and had been through the eighth grade but not to high school. I wondered if she had any plans for the future.

"No'm, I don't know whether I'll get to high school this fall or not. I can't plan about it now."

"No'm, I never thought about wanting to be a teacher. I never knew whether I'd get a chance to be educated, so I've never given it any thought."

"Yes'm, I suppose I will get married some day. That's one reason why I never thought much about getting an education: if I get married, then it would be all wasted."

"No'm, I don't think my mamma and daddy would want me to go away from home to work."

Ethel was a great girl of fifteen, in the eighth grade at the grammar school. Her mother kept a very strict watch over her. Ethel was never seen at parties at the Folk School unless the whole family came. In fact, she seldom went anywhere except to school and Sunday School.

"Yes Ma'am," her mother was saying to me one day, when we were talking about the young folks in the community. "It's a real struggle to drive out of my children's minds the ideas they get after an hour of being over there at school with girls like that Margaret Bennett (who had an illegitimate baby the following year). They've all got the marrying idea. Why, even little Martha Hill has it now. Yes, that's all she thinks about."

"My niece, you know, Mary (eighteen), is mighty thankful now that I persuaded her to be sane and sensible. She told me just the other day she realized how lucky she was now that she hadn't run off and married any old man. That's what she wanted to do, a while back."

A mother: "I've been wishing those people from Florida up there in the Knowlton cottage would take an interest in Paul. He's been doing little jobs for them. I declare, if they liked him and wanted to take him back to Florida when they went, I wouldn't care. I'd let him go. Hit might be the making of him. There's absoluely *nothing* for a boy around here."

Conversation between two Summerville women:
"I hear that Jeweldine's back again—Farmer's granddaughter —the Ulys Farmers that live down there just outside of Piedmont.

"They just got back from Florida. I heard they went there so Jeweldine wouldn't marry this boy. They put her in a girl's home."

"But if her daddy had done as he ought, she wouldn't be like she is; he run away with another woman before Jeweldine was born."

"Well, if the boy is like the one who married my cousin, hit won't do no bit of good to take Jeweldine away. Why my aunt and uncle, they took my cousin on a train like this mornin' and he took a train like this evenin' and followed her right along, and when they got there he married her and come right back with her that day, before her mother and daddy knew anything about it."

"If they can just keep her from gettin' married till she's about twenty-one, she'll be thankful. She'll realize then. Why, she's so little, and she can't do nothin' around the house."

"She's tried three times to get married. Once at Christmas she said she was going to the Christmas party, but she didn't and they caught them. I guess they weren't able to get a license."

A mother: "Yes, Helen's visiting her sister up in Chicago, didn't you know? Oh, I want her to stay up there so bad. May says they'll arrange to give her a business course. But Helen gets so homesick. She writes she wants to come back. I never did know such a girl for hating to be away from home."

Helen came back.

A neighbor: "Did you know the lights was on at the schoolhouse Friday night? I was *told* that the two MacLaughlin girls and J. P. Smith and Duncan Gordon spent the night there. When it's warm weather I've heard those four go to a cave down there near Horsetail Falls to spend the night. They have it all fixed up comfortable like a house."

A member of the Community Council: "No, you won't get Frances to come to these meetings. (She was supposedly the representative from the Young People's Club.) She told me she's afraid she'll have to say something if she comes, so she stays home."

A neighbor: "Last week those boys went over to Bullock's Camp again and let the water out of the swimming pool and threw rocks at Mr. Bullock. Same bunch that was over there last fall and went swimming in the pool one night and defiled it so it had to be all cleaned out. They're mean, I tell you."

An eighteen-year-old girl: "Why do I stay here? Well, if I could get a job, I guess I'd go away. But I really like it here, better than any place I've been. Lots of the girls would rather stay here and wouldn't go away even if they had the chance—girls like Louise Smith and Bertha Priest. I don't know why."

(Louise Smith and Bertha Priest, unlike the girl who was speaking, had never been to high school, and belonged to the shy, self-secluding set of young people in Summerville.)

When the nursery school was located in the public school building, there was just a thin wall separating it from the main school room. Whenever we heard any noise or disturbance in that other room beyond the wall, the voice of Dillard Ladd was sure to be in the center of it, swaggering, tough, raucous, defiant. Dillard was a gangling youngster of about fourteen, in the seventh grade, who tried to make life miserable for the young teacher.

His own life at home, I was told by one who often visited there, was far from pleasant—a matter of the adults and grown sisters nagging at him to do this, do that, just like a child. To himself, Dillard was a grown man.

The schoolteacher, in dismay, early in the morning: "Miss Lewis, my cloakroom's just completely torn up. The extra chairs are all thrown around and half the things are lying outdoors, and that nice little clay vase Caroline made is all smashed. Do you know anything about it? When I locked up after the P.T.A. meeting last night everything was all right. It must have been those two big boys of mine who were at the meeting—they must have gone around there afterwards."

Virginia is eighteen, one of the girls who has been to high school and, incidentally, one whose parents have not always lived in Summerville. She is one of ten children and her father has been off W.P.A. for months, but Virginia always manages to make herself look attractive. It would be very hard to distinguish her, and the other girls of this "set" who have been to the high school, from the well-dressed, well-groomed, poised, modern young high school girls of almost any American city.

Now that Virginia is out of school, she has landed a job with the N.Y.A. at a resident camp several miles from Summerville. She comes to the Folk School one night, during her time off, to tell us all about life at the camp.

"There's one girl there who is so *green*. We went to meet the bus one night and went into the cafe while we waited. She wouldn't even get a Coca Cola! (Giggling.) And when we got back to the house she told the others the kind of dancing they'd been doing at the cafe was something like square dance two-stepping. (Helpless giggles.) Oh my, she's green!"

Charles was sixteen, at least six feet tall, and was finishing the eighth grade at the grammar school, one of the few boys to reach that educational height. But shortly before graduation the young, girlish-looking teacher expelled him. He had refused to take from her the whipping which she felt he deserved because of a repeated misdemeanor having to do with dawdling out on the playground and not coming in on time.

"No'm," he said to me when I talked to him about it, "I ain't never taken a whippin' from her and I don't intend to."

It was a deadlock. The teacher insisted, and Charles firmly maintained that he could not and would not submit to being whipped by her.

He never graduated.

A mother: "You'll have a hard time, I'm afraid, Miss Lewis, finding any girl to help you with the nursery school now. Most of the young folks have to help in the gardens in the summer."

A neighbor: "A bunch of those older boys who weren't going to school tore down the girls' toilet at the schoolhouse on Hallowe'en. And they say that Alf Henderson and his gang used to loll around and drink on the back porch of the school and break their empty bottles there—till the teacher found out and put a stop to it. Just didn't have anything better to do. Like the girls after they'd finished school. Used to parade up and down the road out there with a lot of boys and not one of 'em fit to marry. Things was pretty flat for them, I guess, after all they'd had to do in school, and all the parties and picnics their teacher was always havin' for them."

Miss Justus, the former schoolteacher: "No, not many of the Summerville children were able to finish high school. They'd come back from Dyersville and say to me, 'The teachers don't care anything about us. They don't give us any help. . . . We're lonesome up there.'

"They were used to my kind of school where I constantly was trying to fill them with ambition and inspiration and help them more like a mother than a teacher. If I could have had the same influence on them in high school that I had in grammar school, I think I could have helped a lot more of them to finish. They didn't get enough encouragement at home, and at home no one was able to help them with their lessons. I did have night classes for a while to help a number of them in their first year Latin and Algebra. But somehow even this wasn't enough to encourage them to go on. Of course, *some* did."

Mildred, eighteen, had just given birth to a baby. The story I heard was that the man in the case was forced by another girl's father to marry his daughter before Mildred had a chance.

"But folks won't be hard on her," I was told, "if she settles down and goes straight and works hard to support her baby and help her family."

Two boys, Mark and John—neighbors, not brothers—left on the motorcycle before breakfast. They were off to seek their fortunes in that Land of Promise, land of fruit to be picked, that tempts so many young Summerville boys—Florida.

Mark's older brother had been down there for several months, regularly employed. And Alexander had taken his new young wife down with him on his motorcycle. (Not that every Summerville boy owned a motorcycle! These two happened to be the only ones.) They had landed temporary work in a drug store. But no one would have been surprised to see them rolling in any day, returning to their own kind of life on the loved, familiar mountain, as so many of the young people eventually returned. David had come back from Chicago, Ralph from Detroit, Annie from Nashville and Birmingham, and the two boys who had tried Berea College had also come back home to the mountain.

"What do you do in the afternoons at home?" I asked one of my N.Y.A. girls.

"Nothing much. There ain't nothing much to do. Just sit around and play with the baby."

A neighbor: "Yes, that Myrtle Turner's a queer girl. She ain't spoken to no one but her sister-in-law for a whole year. If you come into her house she'll hide away—curl up in the bed covers or go off down cellar. She's a smart, bright girl, too. She can cook and make things with her hands, and takes nice care of her clothes. Sometimes she'll take a notion to bake a cake and then she goes into the kitchen and shuts the door. Everybody else knows that's a sign to keep out. Sometimes she bakes a chocolate and sometimes a cocoanut cake, or both, and no one touches them except when she cuts the pieces herself. She'll cut three pieces, take one herself and go off and eat it, and leave the other two on the plate. Then her mother and sister take those two pieces; but they wouldn't dream of taking any unless Myrtle cut it for them!"

P.T.A. President: "Have you heard that Hazel's gone back to high school to finish up her last year? Her mother's so proud. I always did tell Hazel that she couldn't expect to get any job better than scrubbing floors unless she had a high school education first."

Pauline was about to be married. Everyone was glad about it. Pauline was a hard-working girl devoted to her illegitimate baby. And now a young man who was divorced from a former wife was going to marry her. They expected to live in Pauline's home. There was no other place.

Everyone was glad—everyone, that is, except Pauline's old grandmother who insisted: "Hit ain't right to marry a man who has a living wife. Hit just ain't right."

The Young People's Class at Sunday School seemed to consist chiefly of the high school set. When the high school set predominated, the shyer young people tended to stay at home, and when a teacher managed to build up a large class of the latter, the high school boys and girls were not so much in evidence. The two groups didn't mix very well.

It was a beautiful sunny day. The "class," which on this day consisted of only four or five young people, sat outside on the steps, chatting and laughing. They had all been out dancing together at one of the cafes the night before and this morning had plenty to talk about which didn't exactly fit in with the Sunday School lesson. One suspects that the chief reason they came to Sunday School was to see each other again, and wind up the threads of the night's escapades. However, when the teacher asked for reading aloud from the Bible, no one observing could possibly have complained of inattention or lack of respect or seriousness on the part of any one of the young people.

A year or so later, there happened to be a fairly large class of the less "sophisticated" young people at Sunday School—though that does not mean that they came for strictly religious purposes, either. In fact, it looked as if Francis Scott had suddenly taken to coming to Sunday School so that he could see Ethel Bennett. Where else was it possible? Ethel's mother forbade her to have anything to do with Francis and kept a careful watch over her, yet insisted on her attending Sunday School.

Ethel was just beginning to curl her hair these days. Straight ends stuck out awkwardly among the ones that had curled up more successfully. She sat there in the back row of the Sunday School class, giggling and whispering with the other fifteen- and sixteen-year-old girls, while an elderly teacher read the lesson and exhorted the young folks more or less at random in a remote and Biblical language.

A couple of our neighbors had been talking for some time of showing us the old stagecoach road down the mountain, which had figured so largely in the lives of many of the Summerville residents. When they spoke of it there was always a fondness in their voices.

And indeed it was a very beautiful road, as we discovered on that June Sunday when we took the hike down, though now it could hardly be called "road." It was not much more than an overgrown path, winding along through luxuriant growth, under magnificent old black walnut trees such as could no longer be found on the top of the mountain.

There were one or two fine old cabins here and there along the way, too, weathered and beautiful old structures of hand-hewn logs, still lived in. One cabin that we passed looked quite new. As we walked by, a young girl came to the doorway and stared at us. "She's a Sanders, kin to the Sanders down in the Cove where we're a-goin'," our neighbor explained. "One of the first houses ever built on this road used to stand right there. The Laynes built it and lived in it for years and years. This new one was put up for Joe Clark, but he moved out because he claimed he was haunted by Mrs. Matt Layne's ghost."

Unexpectedly the road brought us out into a little clearing, halfway down the mountain. We could look across a hedge of vines to a field, and there among the trees beyond the field stood a small, solitary log cabin, growing out of the land as it were, with its porch under the sloping roof open to the wide view of the valley far below and the wooded plateau rising on the other side.

The peaceful and remote quality of the place made us talk softly and walk rather slowly and gingerly as we crossed the field and approached the beautiful little cabin. Our neighbor assured us, however, that it was neither deserted nor haunted but was simply the house Lem Starling had built for himself. Sometimes he lived in it and sometimes he stayed with his parents up in Summerville. He was a boy who loved the mountain and wanted his own house in a place of his own choice.

Lem Starling—why, I knew him. I had seen him fairly recently over at the Folk School. He had been doing some stone work for us; his father was a stone mason and the boy had learned the trade from him. He was just a youngster, not more than nineteen or twenty at the most.

He wasn't at home, so we walked around admiring the workmanship in his house. For quite a while we sat on his little porch, looking down over the mountain into the valley, and thinking that Lem had certainly found the choicest spot in miles around for the home of his own making.

Ed was lucky enough to land a steady job in a store in Chattanooga. He and Hazel got married as soon as he knew this job was to be permanent. She had a ring and a shower—unlike Dotty who had eloped through the cornfield after years of secret courtin' with notes left out under the stone in front of the coal shed— but neither of them had had a church wedding. In fact, all of the young folks seemed just to go up to Dyersville to the courthouse.

After a month or so of married life in Chattanooga, Ed and Hazel appeared back up on the mountain. Ed had given up his job. He had found that he could make more over at Hillsboro. So they moved in with Ed's mother and father, and every day Ed made the long trip over to Hillsboro and back. Soon Hazel found a job for herself too, in one of the Piedmont cafes.

Thus married life began for two of the younger generation.

Adolescence brings the urge for independence and adult status, and in Summerville there are not many ways in which this urge can be satisfied. There are not jobs enough to go around for the fathers of the families, to say nothing of regular employment for the young people. House and farm work are not extensive enough to demand much of anyone's time and energy all year round.

As we have seen, frequently the fifteen- and sixteen-year-olds, already thinking of marriage, find themselves still struggling on in grammar school, like children. And when they finish grammar school, or drop out, what is there for them to do, to fill the hours?

"Courtin' " is a difficult matter to negotiate in the small cabins, and is restricted and frowned upon by some parents anyway. Yet courtin', of course, is what the majority are most interested in, with the result that after secret meetings in the woods, not a few unmarried girls in their teens find themselves with babies on their hands.

Marrying and setting up housekeeping in a cabin of one's own are almost entirely out of the question. These young people look around them and see the land already considerably divided up. Who can build for them a cabin on the corner of the family acres? Their grandfathers could parcel out land a generation ago—Uncle Mac built three small houses for his sons back of the big house where he reared his eight children—but the fathers now have no such resources.

Frustrated, bored, with no jobs and no money, treated like children yet feeling grown up, a good many of the adolescent boys become defiant, destructive—"mean," as they are described in Summerville.

There are few community activities of any sort to enlist the enthusiasm of these young people. The Folk School has, from time to time, encouraged clubs, athletics, attendance at the School's regular terms for working people, and responsible participation in adult activities such as the Community Council, the union, and the classes in whittling, pottery, and singing. A few of the young people have responded. But the Folk School, concerned with the whole Southern labor movement, has seldom had the time, facilities, and personnel to enable it to concentrate on this community problem as it would like to.

Of course, a good many young people have tried to break away and hunt for jobs and independence elsewhere, but always many have returned, perhaps finding the outside world too unfamiliar, too difficult to cope with.

And undoubtedly there are many of this young generation, especially among those who have never been to high school, who will probably never have the courage to leave Summerville of their own accord at any time, for any reason.

For it begins to appear that the placidity of childhood, with its limited experience of conflict and contact and its comparatively easygoing, indulgent routine, may not have given these adolescents a foundation of sufficient strength and breadth and elasticity to sustain them in meeting their new problems. Even the demands for restraint that these youngsters have encountered during childhood, involving respectful attitudes to elders and "proper" behavior (in which sexual curiosity supposedly has had no existence) could hardly be called demands for *self*-restraint, *self*-control.

Of course, one recognizes the very formidable obstacles in the way of these young people. One recognizes, too, that adolescents almost anywhere have their difficulties. But even so, one wonders why adolescent defiance in Summerville takes such destructive forms in many cases; why adolescent restlessness so often fails to work itself out in ways that might lead to more or less satisfactory solutions of the new problems—in other words, why so many drop out of high school, why so many girls find themselves with babies to care for and no husbands to help support them, why so many who have tried the outside world choose to return to the hopeless poverty of the mountain.

One looks around at the adults, too, even those who grew up under much less trying economic conditions, and though greatly admiring their militant, independent spirit, wonders why many of them are so hot-tempered, so quick to flare up and become involved in petty disagreements, why they are so frequently at bickering odds with their neighbors over such small matters. Is it possible that the adolescents who weather their troubles more successfully and the adults who do not have so much of the "mountain feud spirit" in them may be those whose childhoods included not only more contact with a wider world but also more conflict and more experience in making the adjustments leading to resolution of conflict?

WHAT DOES IT MEAN?

❀❀❀❀❀❀❀❀❀❀❀❀❀❀❀❀❀❀❀❀❀❀❀

WHAT IS this "childhood placidity"?

Can we trace its origins, now that we have watched these children working, playing, eating, sleeping, obeying, disobeying up there on their mountain top? Can we understand why they are less active than the roof-top children in New York? Why their play lacks intensity? Why they "mind" so easily? And especially why there are so few of the resisting, striking, crying-in-rage Davids among them, and so few of the brilliant Stephens?

Before we make a complex matter out of something that might have a number of simple ingredients, let us turn back to the picture of the Summerville children in school, remember them digging, swinging, rolling tires around, or just sitting, in the spacious shaded yard behind the house. "Spacious"—that word, as any teacher or mother knows, is a blessed word. When children who have been cooped up, find space to expand in, shout in, and run about in without having to bump up against their fellows or overseers at every turn, conflicts and troubles are almost certain to become less apparent.

It is true that the "school room" itself down in the Tennessee mountains was a smaller one than any Harriet Johnson child had to endure. But the outdoor space was almost limitless, in comparison with the very small, walled-in roof that was David's playground. Johnnie May and J.W. not only had the large schoolyard, but the woods and the brook, the adjoining grove, and the winding roads, all of them free and open for exploration.

And of course their life at home had this same quality of physical spaciousness about it, at least for the six or seven warm months of the year. In at the front door, out at the back with a run and a bang—down to the barn, out to the garden, where and when they please. Whereas David must stay inside his apartment, which in some cases does not afford much more room for expansion than a Summerville cabin, unless and until some adult can pilot him safely down the hazardous streets to the park, where human beings cling to a spot of greenery like ants swarming about a stray drop of syrup. True, David will probably have three months of relative country freedom in the summer time, but three months, compared with nine of restriction, seem but a drop in the bucket. And we must remember that it is during his restricted months that we have seen him, at the Harriet Johnson Nursery School.

As simple a thing as space to play in, then, both at home and at school, and comparative freedom to run around in that space, may partially account for the peacefulness of our Summerville children.

But it was not only the spaciousness of the set-up that contributed to the relative lack of friction with which the mountain children played. The shyness that hung over so many of them for so long prevented them from any group play at all, much of the time. Shy Anna kept to herself, shy Virginia stuck to her one familiar playmate. When children are not trying to take part in the same games, of course there will not be the conflicts that arise out of situations where there are many hands and feet in the same place, many actors and not enough parts, many egos and only one scheme of things.

I have said that the Summerville children usually lost their shyness, as time went on, which is true. But our school had no starting and stopping points, no new terms or long vacations. The enrollment was likely to be a shifting thing. Children came and went. There was never a time when there were not shy children among those who had learned to feel at home.

And another consideration which may seem to be a superficial one, yet may very well have a bearing on the question of the origin of "placidity," is that of climate. The sun that beats down on those Southern mountains is apt to be a wilting one, five months out of the year. It is true that the Southerners themselves consider this mountain climate an ideal "resort" climate, because of the cool nights. But to one from the North, even the prospect of a cool evening ahead does little to alleviate the misery of the penetrating, hot dampness that seeps into everything during the daytime, leaving human beings feeling as wilted as the damp towels hanging there on a line where they will not dry. It seems not unlikely that the Summerville habit of afternoon porch-sitting —idle sitting—may be one that has sprung from the lassitude engendered by the summer heat. It must be remembered that the Summerville Nursery School was always in session during these hot months, as well as during the cold, whereas the picture of the Harriet Johnson children in school is largely one framed in moderate, brisk, or even very cold weather.

And what about the winters in Summerville? Here again, I think that conditions may have conspired to shape less active children. There is no such thing as central heating in a Summerville cabin—home or school—except in a very literal sense. The "central heat" is the heat that comes from the stove in the middle of the room, and if you want to keep warm, you must stay near that stove. Summerville cabins are not built to keep out the cold; and cold rain, cold ice, and snow and frost and fog do come to the mountain in the winter. The summer habit is one of exhausted sitting on the porch. The winter habit is one of cold huddling close to the stove.

When winter came to the mountain during the first year of the nursery school, I scarcely knew what to make of it when the children headed for the stove immediately upon entering and seemed content to pull up chairs and sit there looking at books— or just sitting—for as long as a half hour or forty-five minutes. But they were cold, and placid sitting by the stove was what they were accustomed to in the winter.

Many Summerville children, even when they seemed to be quite warmly dressed, had little resistance to the cold. I had to give up the idea of an outdoor program during most of the winter months. The shivering, weeping little troupe could not stand it, even on days that seemed to me quite bearable. In fact, in Summerville the tables were turned. It was I who did not notice the cold, whereas at the Harriet Johnson Nursery School I had frozen miserably on the roof while sturdy children, muffled up in great snowsuits, played on happily, oblivious to the weather.

The question comes to mind at once, is not health perhaps the very central issue? May not the differences in energy, resistance, and physical well-being that exist between David and J.W. account to a great extent for the differences in their school behavior?

We have seen that Summerville children do not always get the right food, at the right times. " 'Taters, biscuits, gravy," might be almost any child's description of his breakfast. We have seen that the children seldom take naps in the daytime, and that nighttime sleep is often irregular in hours and crowded in its nature. Furthermore, we know that bad tonsils and chronic colds receive little attention.

Even as babies, Johnnie May and J.W. did not always get the sleep they should have had, and certainly did not receive the correctly guided, well-balanced feeding that David and Stephen undoubtedly were given. And let us consider their mothers. It is impossible for us to say just what the effect of their own poorly balanced diet may be on the intra-uterine growth of their children, but that there must be some effect, and probably a not entirely desirable one, would hardly be denied. Nor is it just a question of the mother's diet. Summerville women frequently resume their housework only a week after childbirth, seldom stay in bed when they are ill. Their life is a hard one physically, including in many instances a good deal of carrying of water from long distances. Summerville women age young.

These physical factors, as well as aspects of the life in Summerville such as the general slow tempo and the absence of a good deal of social activity, must have a certain biochemical effect on the organisms exposed to them, a "slowing down" effect. This "slow tempo" is a thing that never fails to attract the attention of the outsider who comes to the Southern mountains. In my own experience it impressed me as a lack of time sense. There seemed to be no need to be "on time"; the exact hour did not have much importance. Summerville people were either hours too soon or hours too late. When I first opened the nursery school, I was of course unaware of this characteristic and confidently set the opening hour at 8:30. I soon learned, however, that some of the children would begin to assemble at the door as early as 7:30. (This did not mean that there had been a rush to get them there! The whole family had been up since 5 or 5:30.) And when, on a few occasions, I did not have the use of the car and had to ask members of families to come and call for their children "at twelve o'clock," I might as well have mentioned any old hour, way beyond twelve.

The formal expression always used when a caller is about to depart is "What's your hurry?" This has become a rote phrase, just as we say "Come again," but undoubtedly there's a reason behind it.

It seems very likely that organic differences between David and J.W. are rather fundamental. At the same time, we must be careful to avoid picturing the mountain children as poor, starved, undernourished little waifs, wobbling on rickety legs. There may be such children in the Southern mountains—there are one or two right in Summerville—but generally speaking that is not at all the impression these children give. According to the weight charts distributed by the Department of Labor, very few of the Summerville children are underweight. The fact that they seem small compared with the Harriet Johnson children is because the latter are oversize and overweight, according to these same tables.

Nor is the diet itself as unbalanced as it might be, if we look closely into it. Certainly many children do not get enough milk, fruit, eggs, but on the other hand there is a good deal of consumption of cabbage, corn, turnip greens, "poke salad," and, especially among the children, raw sweet potatoes. It has even been suggested that the twig-chewing so common among children and adults alike may supply a source of vitamins. (A Summerville woman with a little twig protruding from her mouth is as familiar a sight as the lady with the cigarette in Greenwich Village. Most Summerville women "dip snuff," but very few smoke.)

During the whole two and a half years of the nursery school, we never had to close down because of a contagious disease epidemic, though a few families went through measles, mumps, and whooping cough. Many children dripped with colds for months, and digestive upsets were rather frequent, yet on the other hand there were comparatively sturdy children who scarcely ever missed a day of school during the entire time. As we have seen, children in Summerville live an outdoor life for many months out of the year; they run around barefoot and rather thinly clad in all weathers except the very coldest. It is probable that many of them develop a certain hardiness.

Though physical condition and organic make-up may indeed play an important part in the picture of David and Stephen vs. J.W. and Johnnie May, it seems unlikely that they tell the whole story. How much of the contrast can be ascribed to differences in intelligence?

I hesitate to speak with any certainty when we begin to talk about intelligence. What we are referring to at present when we use this word are the Intelligence Quotients as measured by the Stanford-Binet tests. Our difficulty lies not only in the fact that these tests are probably rather inappropriate measuring rods for isolated mountain children, but also in the fact that such tests measure not native intelligence alone, but native intelligence as it has been developed by environmental influences. This has been strikingly demonstrated by a number of investigators recently who have found, in testing Southern mountain children, that almost invariably scores are lower among older children than younger—indicating, probably, that the older ones have not found sufficient stimulus in their environment to foster the development of intelligence.

On the other hand, intelligence does not depend entirely upon the influences at work upon it. According to what we know at present about the possibilities of raising intelligence scores through environmental change, it seems unlikely that our Summerville four-year-old, with his good average score of 98 or 100, could very easily attain the 135, 146 or even 168 of the Harriet Johnson child, even if from the moment of birth he had been exposed to the same influences. But even here we must speak tentatively. Experimental data are lacking, and the moment of birth is, after all, far too late to begin with our influences.

Regardless of the fact that the scores of the two groups cannot be considered to represent irrevocable and final judgments of intelligence, as they stand the children who grow up in the mountain community seem to achieve no more than average heights, at least in the kinds of abilities that are measured by the Stanford-Binet tests, whereas the Harriet Johnson children frequently reach scores that place them in the ranks of the genius.

It would, of course, be a mistake to attribute the problems presented by the Harriet Johnson Davids entirely to the fact that they are brilliant children. The child in my own group whose score was the highest—and it was a phenomenally high mark—was in no way unstable, hyperaggressive, difficult, unhappy. Quite to the contrary, he was a little boy whose gifts touched every side of his life, emotional and social as well as mental.

At the same time, if we conceive of intelligence in terms of the mental energy that is available, and remember that it takes a certain amount of intelligence even to become aware of the life round about and of problems in that life, it seems to follow that we might reasonably expect to find brilliant children livelier, more self-assertive, more inquisitive—and consequently at times more difficult to handle, more apt to clash with the adults who have to control them—than those who are dull.

This does not mean that we can call the Summerville children "dull." Certainly they appear to be less brilliant than the Harriet Johnson children, but their intelligence scores do not at all justify an assumption that their level of intelligence is so low as to preclude any awareness of difficulties in their lives or possibility of absorption in any emotional problems.

Lower intelligence may indeed enter somewhat into the picture, but at the same time it seems more likely that if J.W. appears to be less troubled, less driven to fight against restrictions than David, it is probably because the circumstances of his life really give him less occasion to feel this way, and less freedom to express such feelings when he does have them. We cannot think of him as a child who is too dull to sense his fate and rebel against it.

Health and organic constitution, play space, climate, intelligence, all have an important bearing on J.W.'s personality. But no less important are these central facts about his life: he is not only a child whose behavior toward adults is controlled by fairly strong taboos, but he is probably a comparatively untroubled child during his early years.

Yes, in spite of his acquaintance with drunkenness in the neighborhood and occasional quarrels or tempests of "cussing" in his home. It seems likely that his knowledge of this side of his parents' life may but cement more firmly his feeling of belonging to the adult world, of being excluded from nothing. Apparently he learns to accept these manifestations, when they are not the symptoms of a fundamental schism in the relations of his parents, as part and parcel of adult life. Our Buddy tells us matter-of-factly, "My daddy and mother cuss all the time whenever they get mad." He seems to show as little emotion or wonderment or distress over the fact that they get mad sometimes as he does when he tells us of some other family event of a different nature, such as, "Mother swapped her pocketbook for my brother's rooster and we're gonna kill it and eat it tomorrow," or when he reports of the man who lives down near his grandfather's house, "Gosh, he's drunk all the time."

Thus we think of J.W. as a comparatively untroubled child, in spite of knowledge of and exposure to things that might trouble a more protected child suddenly stumbling upon them, and in spite of the poverty which keeps his family at times alarmingly close to destitution. But even the extreme poverty of this Summerville, this straggling community situated upon a bad soil, is probably less devastating to its inhabitants than poverty can be in the slums of a large city, for instance.

I have said that Summerville people live close to destitution, but they do not actually become homeless, or starve to death. These families own their small cabins and the plots of ground they are built upon—and rarely pay taxes, I should add. A recent list of delinquent taxpayers published in the county newspaper covered 900 names, and it is well known that the tax law regarding collection of delinquent taxes has not been used for over twenty years.

Potatoes will keep people from actual starvation, and potatoes will grow in this soil. Then, too, there have been at times such helps as free surplus commodities distributed by the Department of Public Welfare. These often consist of flour, grits, beans, butter, prunes, raisins, canned milk. Of course, the amounts proportioned to a family, averaging about $3.65 a month, are not great, not anywhere near enough to live on, but certainly they are a help. And in a place like Summerville there are always kinfolk to stand by in an emergency, kinfolk who will take you in and help you out as much as they can, even when the house is already crowded to overflowing with children to be clothed, fed, and crowded into the beds at night.

Furthermore, most of the parents of these Summerville children have always known this hard life. At the time when they were marrying and setting up housekeeping the mines had already closed down. These young parents scarcely know what an easier life would be like.

I do not mean to minimize the very real difficulties of living in a futureless place like Summerville, but merely to point out that the children, though they may go ragged, do not go really hungry or homeless, nor are their parents riddled with the kind of insecurity that attacks those who suddenly lose their wealth and have no cabin or piece of land to fall back on. We can still say that J.W., though he lives in poverty-stricken Summerville, is probably a comparatively untroubled child.

His babyhood and early childhood, as we have seen, are singularly lacking in what he might feel to be arbitrary demands that he change his habits, or in frustrations of his urgent desires to touch, taste, explore, and grow at his own comfortable pace.

Such frustrations, according to some schools of thought, may give rise to resentment in young children, directed against those who impose the restrictions. Too sudden weaning, too strictly regulated nursing, too early begun and harshly managed toilet training are among the "deprivations" that are thought to mean unhappiness for the baby. And as he grows older, restrictions on his messy play, on the space he wants to expand in, and on his privileges to do the things he sees his parents doing, may give him cause for rebellion. He would scarcely be a normal, healthy child, developing toward independence and self-reliance, if he did not chafe against what he feels to be obstacles to his expanding powers.

In this absence of restriction we may find one of the important keys to J.W.'s apparently compliant, happy life. His long natural babyhood of close physical proximity to his mother; his privilege of suckling at the breast at any time, even long after he is eating the solid foods others eat; the late begun and simply managed matter of toilet training; the few prohibitions relative to "Do not touch this, Do not play there, Do not go in here"; the relatively little insistence on washing, keeping clean; the space in the yard that is his to play about in, and especially the presence of both his parents, and the fact that he is not shut out from their life or their emotions, not deprived of their company day or night, not told that he must stay home, go to bed, keep away— all these things make his young childhood a time of ease. He does not often have to picture his parents as "those grown-up people who can do everything they want to but won't let me do anything."

On the other hand, it would be wrong to assume that all Harriet Johnson children, for instance, who are born in hospitals and are immediately removed from their mothers; who are bottle-fed at regular intervals; who are trained early not to soil their clothing, who are entrusted to nursemaids a good deal of the time, and who do not eat the same food at the same hour or place the parents do; who are put to bed, alone, on a rigid schedule—it would be wrong to assume that on account of these so-called "frustrations" the children exposed to them must *inevitably* develop deep antagonism which fills them with a compensatory need to explode and rebel.

As Karen Horney and others have pointed out,* children can take a good deal of frustration if it is imposed in the right spirit, with love and gentleness and obvious fairness behind it. It is not really "frustration" itself, they say, which is hard on children, so much as a sense of loss of love that follows when parents impose the frustrations thoughtlessly or harshly—though of course some explosions may be expected from almost any child if his self-assertive impulses are not given sufficient rein. If a child's confidence in his parents as consistently loving protectors is shaken, then comes that extremely upsetting feeling of being adrift in a world where there is nothing certain and solid. Then comes "aggressiveness" in the attempt to overcome the terrors.

It is warmth and belongingness, and a sense of confidence in loving, sympathetic, fair treatment that are children's basic needs. There is no reason to believe that a Harriet Johnson child cannot experience this sense of being loved and wanted and justly treated, and that he cannot hold an important and assured place in the family affections. As a matter of fact, the child in the Greenwich Village one-child family is usually one whose advent has been planned, and is therefore welcomed; his presence in the family and his growth and development are matters of devoted interest and concern. Yet it is very probable that some of our rebellious, self-assertive, thumb-sucking Davids may be children who are attempting to compensate for keenly felt deprivations too impatiently and intolerantly enforced in babyhood. Young mothers like theirs, who have become aware that some ways of handling children are approved by psychological thought and other ways are not, may very well become too concerned that they are following the right procedures down to the letter, and may sometimes apply the rules a little too rigidly and unsym-

* Karen Horney, *New Ways in Psychoanalysis* (New York, W. W. Norton and Co., 1939).

pathetically. This is understandable in view of the fact that only comparatively recently have psychologists been recommending a general relaxation of the rules in favor of warmth and gentleness and a more human approach—the very approach, in fact, which Summerville mothers use as a matter of custom, all unaware of "psychology." (This is not to imply, however, that the Summerville mother's "instinct" always guides her aright, and that her complete ignorance of pediatricians' and psychologists' findings has been an unmitigated blessing!)

Clearly, the Summerville child has been spared certain sources of unhappiness which may fall rather easily to the lot of the Harriet Johnson David. In fact, J.W. probably grows through childhood with as full a measure of the safe and comfortable sense of belonging as a child could have, not only because of the easy, unrestricted nature of babyhood, but because other circumstances of his life conspire to build him so solidly into the fabric of the family and community. His life in Summerville where the family is close-knit, where processes of birth and death go on in the home, where to some extent the production of food takes place right there in his own garden or in his own back yard where the hog is killed—this life has some of the integration so characteristic of our preindustrial era, an integration that has been called essential for healthy development.* Needless to say, the circumstances of David's and Stephen's lives are quite different.

Furthermore, the actual physical presence of J.W.'s parents is a reality to him, from early babyhood, when he is constantly being cuddled in someone's arms, up through later years when his dad lets him tag him around. And not only does he see a good deal of his parents, take part in their work and recreation and conversation and troubles, accompanying them to revivals, buryings and "sit-down strikes," but his life with them goes on day after day *in the same place*. He belongs in his familiar home as well as in his familiar family, and is not subjected to the upsetting

---

* James S. Plant, *Personality and the Cultural Pattern* (New York, The Commonwealth Fund, 1937).

experience of frequent moving that apartment-dwelling Davids often have to go through.

Then, too, a Summerville household which does not include both father and mother is rare. Divorce and separation are not very common among these families. The deep sense of loss, the emotional disturbance following upon such separations are not the lot of the Summerville child as often as they are of the Harriet Johnson child. Ernestine, of course, *was* one Summerville child whose timid personality clearly revealed the effects of living in a household where the underlying solid and dependable structure of loving relationships had been shattered. Ernestine's parents were not divorced, but wanted to be. The father was considered by all the rest of the family a worthless drunkard, and the troubles between the parents, I was told, resulted in the mother's illness and a near miscarriage shortly before Ernestine was born. But Ernestine in Summerville was something of an exception. In New York, in the Harriet Johnson Nursery School, the fearful little girl would have found a number of similar playmates among those whose parents were in the process of separating, or those whose family circles included a new step-parent.

Furthermore, the Summerville child almost never has the experience of seeing his loved mother, as well as father, go off to work while he is left to a maid—or succession of maids. Nor is he exposed to the other strains that may grow out of such a household situation. For instance, in a family—a Greenwich Village family—where both parents are working, sometimes with devotion to a "cause," the child may suffer not only from lack of attention but from the high speed and tension that are necessary if both home and cause are to be served. This is a very different picture from the one we have seen in Summerville of mother, grandmother, aunts, children, sitting away the hot afternoons on the porch—and father there also a good deal of the time.

Then, too, a child in this Village household where both parents work may suffer from a too-meticulous worry over every little piece of his behavior which his mother may very well develop when she is at home with him, to compensate for her lack of time with him. (Is this one of the reasons why, in the nursery school, he finds it difficult to brook interference with what he is doing, no matter how legitimate such interference may be? Why he develops the David-like pugnaciousness to adults that is so different from J.W.'s attitude?)

Furthermore, in this Village family which consists of mother, father, child, and maids, there may be difficulties revolving around the question of discipline, difficulties that seldom touch J.W., for whom discipline is usually consistently a matter of clear-cut parental authority, never in the hands of nursemaids. In fact, in the matter of discipline, J.W. and Johnnie May, though whipped, have one distinct advantage. They are never left in any doubt about what is expected of them.

In David's household, on the other hand, the nursemaid in the afternoon may handle him with anything but the lenience and gentleness he is accorded by his parents, and even their leniency may be confusing to him. For David's parents, following the popular swing away from authoritarian control, may be attempting methods which they see very effective in the school but which, transferred into the home, may not work so well, possibly because of the lack of the necessary firmness. The "discipline" in the Harriet Johnson Nursery School is administered by teachers whose manner is so gentle and pleasant that the firmness and quiet assumption of authority behind it may escape the observer. Consequently, at home the Harriet Johnson child may flounder, uncertain of what is expected of him, left too much to his own choices, or to argue with parents who are themselves hazy as to where the basis of authority lies and why.

J.W., of course, misses the educational opportunity that David may have, to learn a gradual adjustment and self-control; and certainly the harshness of whipping, or even the threat of a whipping, may not be the best possible influence on him, as we shall consider later, yet still the certainty of the framework that Summerville discipline provides may very well be a prop to him, an influence making for stability and realistic adjustment to reality.

There are other circumstances in the nature of J.W.'s family life that are a distinct advantage to him. If it is true, as Margaret Mead points out,* that the organization of the family is a factor of prime importance in producing harmoniously developed individuals, then the Summerville family has a good deal to offer. In the first place, the presence of many brothers and sisters tends to obviate extreme jealousies and to eliminate other problems that may confront the only child, such as the problem of learning how to get along with other children. There were very few of the Summerville children who on entering the nursery school were not already well versed in the ways of other children and how to meet them. Among the Harriet Johnson children, on the other hand, there were a number who had seldom played with children of any age, but had spent almost all of their time with adults. No wonder they clung to the skirts of the teacher when they came to school.

A house full of brothers and sisters is a great help to J.W. and Johnnie May. And so, probably, is the presence of many adults. Grandmothers, aunts, uncles, are practically like additional fathers and mothers to turn to. In such households it is not likely that an intensely close relationship will spring up between the child and one adult. The whole pattern of behavior does not revolve around the personality of this adult, her demands, her expectations of the child. There is room to take things easy.

And what about the important question of attitudes toward birth, death, and sex, in these crowded households? It is usually considered that neuroses and personality difficulties are less prone to develop where knowledge of these things is open and the aura surrounding them is matter-of-fact. Is this the case in Summerville?

It cannot be said that the Summerville child's education in sex is an open matter. In fact, he knows a good deal less about the process of birth than do the Harriet Johnson children, whose parents, generally speaking, feel that it is best to tell the truth to

* Margaret Mead, *Coming of Age in Samoa* (New York, William Morrow and Co., 1928).

children when they show sexual curiosity. On the other hand, death is an experience that comes much closer to the Summerville children than to the Harriet Johnson children. Though a burial in Summerville usually takes place on the day of death, children do have the experience of seeing, if only for a few hours, the bodies of those who were once alive, lying right there in their cabins or in the cabins next door. And of course the meaning of burial is well known to them. Buddy saw his grandfather in his coffin, just before the funeral. It was hard for Buddy to realize why they would bury a man in his good clothes—it was clear to him what "bury" meant. "He had on a clean tie and a clean coat. Gosh, I wouldn't mess up clean clothes!"

It is likely, too, that the children are able to talk freely about "peeing" because this is a rather open matter around their homes. Small children use the outdoors frankly for this purpose, and no one expects them to do otherwise.

It may be objected that in such crowded homes, the children are bound to witness sexual intercourse at some time or other, that the question of sex and birth cannot remain a closed book, a safe little story about the doctor, that does not bother them. I am inclined to think that the matter is more carefully guarded from small children than one might suppose. It must be remembered that these are people whose tradition in this respect is a stern Victorian one—they do not have the abandoned, "natural" approach to sex that one might for a moment expect to find among a mountain people. Quite the contrary. They are hedged about with modesty, shame, taboos. One mother told me that she had finally decided to tell her fourteen-year-old daughter that there was about to be an addition to the family. "I hated to do it, but I figured she'd better find out that way than some other way. I told her she must be careful to keep it from the little fellows." And I don't doubt that in some families even bathing and undressing are so arranged that naked bodies of adults are never displayed to the other members of the family. ("Undressing for bed," it must be remembered, does not always mean taking off all one's clothes.)

I think it is quite possible that the majority of small children

may actually not be exposed to the sexual relationship as frequently as one might suspect, if at all, especially since many parents do not even sleep together much of the time, but take turns
sleeping with the children.

I would raise the question, too, whether a child told simply that
the doctor brings the baby really carries around with him as much
of a burden of curiosity as may be possible to a child who has been
told the whole story before his questions have encompassed the
whole act, or a child whose parents, though they have told the
truth because they consider it the enlightened thing to do, may
have done it with embarrassment and confusion. Furthermore,
this child who has been presented with a matter-of-fact treatment of it all is likely to be distressed by the attitude of "For
shame, you shouldn't talk about these things," which is sure to
greet him when he steps outside the bosom of his intelligent
family.

The children in the Summerville nursery school seemed to
speak freely of what they considered the origin of babies without
any sense of shame or mystery or taboo in talking about it. Not
even our most "proper" little girl showed any signs of being
shocked when the children were discussing which doctors
brought them, though she always promptly reported cussing to
me, and hushed children who were talking nonsense at the table.
Nor could I ever detect a sign that the children's curiosity was un-
satisfied. There never seemed to be any further questioning, any
self-consciousness, any embarrassment. In Summerville, I suspect
that this kind of curiosity actually may not develop any further
until the children are past the pre-school age—which probably is
not the case with our lively, highly intelligent Harriet Johnson
children. It is my feeling that J.W. is as secure and untroubled
in his ignorance as David is in his much greater knowledge of the
process, of the parts of the body and their correct names and
functions.

Obviously, however, there is the possibility that some children
may at times witness sexual intercourse, or may develop further
curiosity about the origin of babies. For them there can be only

a deep repression of such interests, in the face of the powerful taboos that will confront them if they ask any questions. And obviously, too, inhibitions and unresolved conflicts concerning the subject of sex probably do become a part of Johnnie May's and J.W.'s personalities as they grow older and still receive no true explanations, no open and frank acceptance of the subject on the part of their parents. But problems of this sort—and indeed problems of any sort—appear to have but a transitory place in the life of our four-year-old J.W. Not only is his own life comparatively free from many of the hurdles common to childhood elsewhere, as we have seen, but the adults around him may be considerably less burdened in some ways than the adults who live, say, in David's household.

At this point it would be easy to stop and glibly describe Summerville in general terms as a "homogeneous culture," a "noncompetitive society," where life flows along smoothly and consequently maladjustments, personal difficulties, are unheard of. Such an attempt at generalization on my part I feel sure would be fraught with error. And yet there is certainly a kernel of truth in both of these assumptions, that homogeneity and a kind of noncompetitiveness are to be found in Summerville to a rather unusual degree, considering that this community is a part of our United States. It seems not unlikely that, as a consequence, Summerville people may be somewhat less harassed with the need to hold up their end of the competitive rope and with the necessity of making choices at every turn than is common in many parts of our country.

For instance, in a Summerville home, the role of the wife is housekeeper and mother; that of the husband, wage earner. It is as simple and as taken-for-granted as that. If a Summerville mother works outside of the home, and occasionally she does find housework and washing to do, it is only because of desperate economic necessity, not because of ambition for a "career." Ask the small children what they want to be when they grow up, and their answers reflect the simplicity, the clear limitations of these roles. A little boy wants to "be a man and milk cows and work." A little girl wants to "be a woman and cook."

Furthermore, the Summerville man and wife grew up in the same community, or in near-by similar communities, went to the same school for about the same length of time, probably went to the same revival meetings. They believe alike in heaven and hell; they vote alike for the same president. Though of course they may differ as to whether or not Johnnie May should be made to take castor oil when Castoria might be just as effective and more pleasant or whether Paul William should stop his smoking, by and large they speak the same language, the language of Summerville, Tennessee—for that is about all that either of them has ever known. It would be extremely difficult to picture the average Summerville home as one in which one parent was an atheist and insisted on treating Sunday like every other day, while the other parent was a devout churchgoer; or where one believed that woman's place was in the home and the other—the woman—longed for a wider world and made every effort to get out in it. Yes, there is a good deal of real homogeneity in a Summerville household.

Is it true that there is no competition in the community? I do not mean to suggest that Summerville people are of a strange breed who do not know what it is to feel this drive to compete with their fellows. In situations where there is something to compete for, I know that they enter in with all the push and coldly calculating selfishness that is supposed to characterize us who live in competitive America.

"Just watch a bunch of pigs," one parent said to me, when he was talking to me about the scarcity of jobs and the way everyone in Summerville went after every little extra bit of ditch-digging that turned up. Undoubtedly Summerville people compete for jobs to supplement their small relief earnings. There is so little work to go around, and jobs are so desperately needed.

But competition for material possessions because of the status and prestige inherent in them—such competition as keeps our many American "Middletown" * residents going at breakneck speed—seems not so characteristic of Summerville. Here status does not seem to be measured so strongly in terms of dollars and cents, fine houses, fine cars, fine clothes. Quite the contrary, the overall and the apron are as decent and honored articles of clothing as anyone could want to have for any occasion. It is true that most Summerville men do own suits of clothes, but overalls are by far the preferred article of wear among them. And the apron among women seems to have assumed an almost symbolic significance. Many women wear one most of the time, even when housework is over. Here is Mrs. Ladd at the schoolhouse, all dressed up for a P.T.A. committee meeting. She is neat and pretty in a Sears Roebuck printed voile dress—but over it she has pinned her inevitable, spotless white apron. And when Mrs. Bennett forgets to take her apron along when she goes up to Dyersville to help with the cooking at the W.P.A. demonstration, she feels it so important to have one that she actually buys a new one up there in the store, though the dress she is wearing is just an old gingham work dress, very washable, and though the funds of the family are in a most precarious state during this long period when her husband is cut off W.P.A.

I indicated that many Summerville people looked down on those who lived in the "Cove," but it should be pointed out that the reason for this could not have been because of the poverty of the Cove people, which was indeed not much more extreme than Summerville's poverty. It must have been because the state of both houses and morals was considered slovenly. Many writers on the Southern mountaineers mention this assumption of equality that is found among the people, this feeling that a man's worth does not depend upon his money, but that there is "status" enough to go around for all, regardless of wealth. Perhaps such descriptions are exaggerated at times. Perhaps Utopian "equal-

* R. S. Lynd, and Helen M. Lynd, *Middletown* (New York, Harcourt Brace and Co., 1929).

ity" is what the writers expect and hope to find and so do find, willy nilly.

I do not believe for a moment that Summerville's residents are never jealous of their neighbors, never involved in any struggle whatever for any kind of status and gratification of vanity. Quite the contrary. The jealousies and rivalries that can spring up at the touch of a match can be very intense and bitter, and may make it practically impossible to carry on any kind of cooperative enterprise. The records of one cooperative gardening attempt are full of such discouraging notations as:

"Mr. C. reported that Mrs. L. did not wish to participate in the cooperative canning of tomatoes due to the fact that Mrs. B. was chairman." "Mr. W. closed the subject of the Cooperative immediately with the statement that he could not cooperate with any project in which the B.'s participated." "They reported that Mr. S. had been drinking and stealing, and would not permit the C. family on the tomato patch, that it was impossible for anyone to work with Mrs. B., and that all refused to be dictated to by Mrs. S."

However, at the same time there is real truth in the observation that rivalry for prestige whose basis is material wealth does not seem to be keen in Summerville. This particular competitive pattern, so familiar to us, does not fit snugly over Summerville's life. Naturally it must be remembered that there is not the same lure to accumulate the material goods of modern life as must exist in places which are under constant bombardment from advertising, radios, movies. Summerville people read very little and do not often see well-stocked modern stores. It is perhaps no wonder that status in terms of "things" has not become a more important part of their code. Indeed, where poverty is so general, such an urge could meet only with frustration.

It has been pointed out that the values which form the basis of competition may be responsible for more friction and confusion in modern life than the competition itself, because these values are not static and dependable at the present time, but are racing along upsetting each other daily, and no one is sure just what is left to cling to. It seems apparent that the process of dislocation of old values is taking place much more slowly in Summerville than in the outside world, and that this may more account for the absence of friction in the life of the place than what we have called lack of competition.

A grandfather, of course, would not agree that life goes on in Summerville today just as it did when he was young. He looks back rather mournfully to the good old days when "it was everybody for somebody else, not everyone for himself like it is now. Folks didn't have much money then, but you didn't need it. If you wanted some meat and didn't have it, you went to the man who butchered a hundred and fifty hogs in one day and told him you wanted some. All right, you worked for the man that day and went home with a side of pork forty or fifty pounds, worth a dollar and a half. It was like that for everything—exchange. And you had to make almost everything. You couldn't run off to stores. And folks don't have the nice Sunday School and school Christmas trees they used to have for children in the old days. Then really nice presents were given. People thought more of making the children happy than anything else."

Yes, of course, there have been changes. But though Uncle Mac laments the passing of the Sunday School Christmas tree, he has no occasion to mourn the passing of Sunday School or religion itself: the Bible is still the word, and heaven and hell are realities. This value, one of the most fundamental of all, has not yet been swept off its feet. It is true that the number of actual devout churchgoers in Summerville is but a handful, except at revival time. But one has the feeling that religion is still there, firm as a rock, for any occasion when it is needed. (The fact that the churches are not filled to overflowing every Sunday in the year, though clearly the people have not turned disbelievers, makes one wonder if Summerville residents actually do not feel the great need for religious support that might be felt in a less isolated, more complex community where the struggle for existence is more highly tinged with both ambition and sense of frustration.)

Nor do parents flock to P.T.A. meetings with questions about what to do about J.W.'s eating, disobeying, thumb-sucking. They have not yet learned to question the advisability of whipping, of unregulated nursing. There were very few in the community who seemed to show any disapproval of the educational system under which a sixteen-year-old boy could be expelled a few days before graduation for refusal to take a whipping from the young woman who was his teacher.

It is true that there are probably more conflicts today between parents and children of the high school set than there were a number of years ago. These children want dates and dancing at night, auto rides. They have been more exposed to the influences of autos, schools, and movies than their parents have, and where the parents retain their strict ideas there is bound to be conflict. Mr. Ladd even went out with his gun one night and procured the safe return of a daughter who had been persuaded to take an auto ride by a young college boy visiting in the neighborhood!

Conflicts of this sort will probably increase as more and more of the Summerville young people go out into "the world," bringing back its ways. For the present generation of parents, however, especially those whose children are of nursery school and school age, we can still say that by and large the even tenure of life and the values underlying it have not been greatly disturbed. Religion, hospitality, respect for elders, marriage and a home literally full of "decent, obedient children"—ideas about the fundamental worth and rightness of these things have not felt the challenge that comes in the wake of literacy, money, movies, advertising, and the other influences of a fast-moving, industrial age.

It is interesting to speculate, too, whether or not Summerville residents are likely to suffer so much from that "impairment of self-confidence" which, according to Horney, takes place as a result of the contradictions in our modern way of living. The Summerville boy, after all, does not grow up to find the adult world a very different sort of place from the one he knew as a child. Parents do not shield things from their children. Buddy knew that a man had chased his father around the house trying to kill him; children know that people get drunk and occasionally violent; they hear their parents talking freely about which neighbors they consider good-for-nothing; they know their dads are constantly struggling for jobs. Their crowded home life does not foster the growth of any illusions about people.

Furthermore, in a community in which all are living in poverty, obviously through no fault of their own but clearly because there are no jobs left in the mines and the timber, men are not so apt to impute their failure to provide for their families to their own personal worthlessness.

Here, too, a boy is rarely pumped full of ambition to go out and startle or conquer the world, or to become President some day—ambitions which are sure to bump up against hard limitations when he actually starts out on his own. Summerville parents realistically have no such plans for their children.

Again I must say that I wish to avoid making sweeping generalizations concerning these "cultural trends," or concerning the pattern of the community as a whole. There are too often individuals who do not fit into these snug descriptions, and there is much room for mistake when an outlander tries to define such an intangible thing as "the nature" of the mountaineer and his life. I am very wary of ascribing too much of the children's placidity to what I have called the homogeneity, the comparative noncompetitiveness, and the stable values and absence of contradictions in the community in which they grow up.

But granting that to some extent there may be a reality in all of these concepts which does reflect back on the children, can we at the same time say that the Harriet Johnson children who live in Greenwich Village experience the very opposite of these factors in their lives? Can we say that their environment is not homogeneous, that their parents are breathless and frustrated with competition, that their homes are torn with the confusions brought about by changing values, that the adults who surround them have lost their confidence in the midst of this contradictory world, and, because of this, many of the children are high strung, fearful, hyperaggressive, unstable?

On the surface, it appears that this may not be so.

Certainly the Greenwich Village inhabited by the nursery school parents is a far cry from Middletown, which typifies competition in our nation. As Caroline Ware has pointed out in her study,* the "Villagers," as distinct from the Italian and other "local" peoples, are comprised of various groups, differing in the way and in the degree to which their members have repudiated old values, yet all in common sharing a disregard, not for money itself, certainly, but for the prestige that is based on possessions and showy expenditure. It would be my guess that the parents of the Harriet Johnson children—the Villagers—are as little concerned with what is called the race of keeping up with the Joneses as are Mr. and Mrs. Smith in Summerville, for reasons that are equally genuine, if not more so. After all, the Smiths could not keep up with the Joneses—say the Dyersville Joneses—if they wanted to. The Villagers could, but do not choose to base their living on these values.

This does not mean, however, that there is no kind of competition for prestige in the Village; that there is no attempt at all to keep up with anyone. As a matter of fact, many of the Villagers would probably recognize that they are competing in at least one subtle race which is a matter of great importance to them—and that is the race of keeping up with the "modern" (though it may be simple) taste of the group in such things as dress and home decoration, and even in the wider realm of reading matter and ideas.

Furthermore, while on the surface the competition for jobs does not seem to be keen, considering that the Villagers hold high positions in professional fields, one certainly cannot claim that the achieving and holding of such positions today is a simple process entirely free from competition and from attacks on security and self-confidence.

And again, though many Villagers have repudiated old traditional values of religion and social position and have succeeded

* Caroline F. Ware, *Greenwich Village, 1920–1930* (Boston, Houghton Mifflin Co., 1935).

in establishing firm new ones, such as cultural values, in their
stead, it is not likely that every family has had this success, nor
can we assume that in many cases the process of repudiation has
gone on without struggle, pain, and bewilderment. Moreover,
among the new values which Villagers are apt to establish is a
concern for the "fullest development of the individual"—a value
which drives and goads them as relentlessly as the money urge
drives others. Drives them to expect a good deal not only of
themselves but also of their children. In a family where there is
but one child and the parents are both highly intellectual, this
may mean that the child is not allowed to take his childhood at
his own normal rate of growth. He is pushed into maturity, into
development of his capacities, especially his intellectual capacities, and into adult interests that are not natural for him.

J.W.'s parents on the other hand, as we have seen, enjoy his
babyhood, are a little bewildered if you mention that his speech
is backward and you wonder what could be done about it, take
school attendance rather lightly, and certainly do not dream of
his future in terms of the professions he may follow or the talents
he may develop.

Furthermore, David's parents, who expect much of themselves
and their offspring, are apt to hang over him, their only child,
with bated breath. In him are all their hopes. And their sense of
personal responsibility for his success is keen because his coming
was no "act of God," no matter of course, as was the coming of
J.W. and his six brothers and sisters. In their very concern, they
may create problems.

No, Greenwich Village may not be Middletown. It certainly
presents less of a competitive and value-upturned picture than
do many areas of our country. But in comparison with a place
like Summerville it would seem to be in many ways a center of
dislocation and ferment.

This is particularly true when we begin to consider the question of the homogeneity of its people. Obviously, there is no simple sort of homogeneity about the backgrounds of the nursery
school families, or about the life of New York City that sur-

rounds them. One parent may bring to her home in the Village a knowledge of life in the Kentucky mountains, the other his experience of years in Paris. That both have strong interests outside of their home goes without saying. The wife frequently has a professional career to carry on along with a homemaking one, or is devoted to some social cause, or to serious study and practice of an art. One parent may be a doctor, a writer, a college professor; the other may be a musician, actor, teacher, book designer, photographer. One may vote the Democratic ticket, the other the Socialist; one may be devoted to Cooperatives, the other uninterested in social reform; the mother may have familiarized herself with modern psychological thought and may have developed real insight into and skill in handling the problems the children present; the father may be less skilled, less tolerant.

Contradictions, and compromises difficult to make, are bound to arise in situations such as these where many points of view, many interests, many choices to be made, all exist under the same roof. Furthermore, a kind of bitter competition with devastating results to the personality may develop in homes where the roles of husband and wife are not clearly set apart in different spheres but where both move about in the world of intellectual and artistic—and remunerative—pursuits. It is not easy for a man in America today, even an enlightened man who theoretically believes in equality between the sexes—to see himself less of a success in his profession than his wife is in hers. Such a situation quite conceivably can arise among Village parents.

Clearly, here in the Harriet Johnson families there may be sources of conflict that do not exist in Summerville families, simply because Summerville people are not exposed to the great variety of experience which is part and parcel of Greenwich Village life.

It seems quite evident that life for a child in a Village home may be complicated by hurdles that are really too high for his limited stride. When and if he is left to tackle them without enough help, he finds himself balked and thwarted, and gives in to rage, kicking at the obstructions or seeking devious means around them. When he comes to nursery school baffled, angry, afraid, we call him David.

However, that is not to say that such hurdles must inevitably fall to the lot of every Harriet Johnson child. We have seen that not all are Davids, that there are even-tempered, happy, stable children in the school, children whose energetic ways and self-assertiveness may be considered "normal" expressions of growing need for independence or of inability to endure too much spacial restriction. This mild kind of rebellion, characteristic of Summerville children too to some extent, is not complicated by deep underlying emotional disturbance. It is necessary to distinguish between the aggressiveness which represents merely a bursting away from the usual childhood restraints and that which is a symptom of maladjustment.

Obviously, many parents have managed to eliminate the particular serious hurdles we have mentioned, or to help the children over them without the accompaniment of undue strain. And obviously, too, there are very positive values in the Village kind of life, values which are denied Summerville children.

If the simple homogeneity of Summerville spares children and adults alike from the necessity of coping with certain problems, undoubtedly the very variety of experience encountered by the Harriet Johnson children in their homes and in the life of New York City develops their intelligence and awareness and deepens their personalities. It must be remembered that Stephen, with his brilliance and talent and insight, comes from a Village home as well as David. In fact, it may be that a certain proportion of seriously troubled, unhappy Davids represents the unavoidable price to be paid for a culture that can at the same time produce the superior Stephens. Remove the conditions that may give rise to David's problems, and what you have left is Summerville with its untroubled, average J.W.'s and Johnnie Mays. Could Stephen find enough in the mountain soil to nurture him? Probably not. But this question will be considered more fully in a later chapter.

If the Village concern for "fullest development" may sometimes result in children who are pushed ahead of their normal rate of growth, on the other hand it may mean wisely chosen experiences that provide the best possible milieu for the flowering of intelligence and abilities and personality. Most certainly the concern and care for health, where not accompanied by over-anxiety, can result in splendid physical foundations. Moreover, if a Village mother who has a career may run the risk of neglecting her children, on the other hand there is the chance that she may bring to her home a good deal more in the shape of a happy, satisfied, expanding personality than she would if she stayed at home but felt that she was stagnating, not living the vigorous, many-sided life she wanted to be living.

If too rigid following of the psychologist's rules and concern over them may lead to mistakes, on the other hand a familiarity with, and real understanding of modern findings may mean that a parent is in many ways helped to provide her children with a sympathetic atmosphere that is a source of great security to them. A mother who understands that it is "natural" for a developing child to strive toward a certain amount of independence, to wrench away from restrictions, will not be inclined to hedge him in all the more when he says "No" sixty times a day, but will try to give him some of the freedom he is pursuing and will probably see many of his "No's" evaporate as a result.

Such an atmosphere of tolerance, of understanding of the reasons back of children's behavior, allows for a gradual growth in *self*-control, a gradual adjustment to the ideas that dominate the adult world of behavior. A child who grows up in such an environment is not asked to accept all at once a full-blown set of parental rules and taboos which may not all make sense to him. He does not need to hide or deny impulses which may seem entirely justified from his immature point of view. There is no room for fear in this kind of atmosphere. A ready and complete "compliance" is not expected of him, but, rather, a gradual growth in understanding, gradual mastery of his unacceptable impulses. If resilience and strength and self-discipline are the outcomes of this kind of training, it is clear that in this respect David and Stephen may be the gainers, J.W. and Johnnie May the losers.

Furthermore, if there is the possibility that David may sometimes be confused by the hazy limitations on his behavior that result from inconsistent discipline administered by too many different people; if the firmness that would help him achieve self-control is sometimes lacking, on the other hand he is never subjected to anything so harsh as a whipping or even a threat of a whipping. He probably never has to fear that a "Big Black Nigger" or a Boogerman will get him if he is not good.

I have said that the Summerville children are not often physically mistreated, that on the whole the whippings they get are few and far between and seem to be accepted rather matter-of-factly. It is obvious that Summerville children are not so cowed by their whippings, so filled with fear that they leap to obedience at their parents' slightest command. Many of them learn how far they can go in defiance and do not hesitate to ignore parental admonitions.

At the same time, it is difficult to see how whippings can fail to leave marks of fear and timidity on certain of the most sensitive children—especially if these whippings happen to descend rather irrationally, without reasonable provocation, as may sometimes happen. (It is probably not harsh punishment in itself which brings the blight of undue timidity into the child's personality, but *unpredictable* harsh punishment.)

Elsie was one of the shyest children who ever came to the nursery school. It was her mother who said to me one day, "You can't scare Buddy like you can Elsie. If I get a switch he'll just get one too. But take a switch to Elsie and she'll do anything I say for a week." Furthermore, a playmate of Elsie's reported to me one day that Elsie's dad was "mean" and "rough." "He'll whip Elsie for almost nothin'—he makes her hush so he can listen to the radio."

Was Elsie shy because of this harshness?

By and large, it seems to me that the excessive shyness of most of the Summerville children has its roots in another explanation: Summerville adults, too, are excessively shy. They have that reserve in the presence of strangers that is usually labeled "English." Furthermore, their lives are lived in an enclosure where all dress alike, speak alike, think alike, and there is little opportunity to meet those who differ from their pattern. The heterogeneity of a place like Washington Square, for instance, where our small Villager out playing in the afternoon will make the friendly acquaintance of a neat, well-dressed, well-mannered twelve-year-old boy who has a big bicycle, and then immediately following, of a rather unkempt-looking, dark-faced, friendly Italian boot-black who speaks English only brokenly—such heterogeneity does not exist in Summerville to prepare J.W. for easy contact with people who are not quite like himself. The world of what is "Known," a world in which he can move about safely without fear, is much smaller for him than for David and Stephen.

It was noticeable that the Summerville young people who had been to the high school in Dyersville, and even younger children who had learned to feel more or less at home at the Highlander Folk School where they had had the opportunity to meet quite a variety of people, were a good deal less shy than those who had not had these contacts.

At the same time, we can ask, would our small David in Washington Square go walking off down the sidewalk so willingly, holding the grimy hand of the big rough-looking, strange man beside him, if he had known sudden, irritated harshness from his father, or if he had a dim picture of a Boogerman lurking in the back of his mind?

This seems to be a matter for conjecture, not proof. My own guess is that if J.W. and some of his more sensitive playmates had never had to fear harsh whippings at the hands of adults, nor vague terrifying creatures lying in wait with punishments, they might possibly not find it quite so difficult to warm up to the outlander. True, they might occasionally strike their teacher and call her "Miss Stink." (Though probably not unless the "moral" restraints, the powerful taboos branding such behavior as "terrible," were also relaxed or changed.)

David, unlike J.W., has few menacing shadows trailing his conduct. His teachers, and by and large his parents, believe that nothing is to be gained by shaming or harshly punishing him because of his behavior, even if this behavior includes attacks on them and others—attacks which, as we have seen, do stem from urgent need, and represent his ways of trying to battle against obstructions that rise too high for him, whether these obstructions take the form of unreasonable standards for achievement, too many restrictions on freedom, intruding stepfathers, or terrible fears that mother's love is deserting him.

This is not to say that he is left to "run wild," to trample on adults and children as he pleases. As a matter of fact, a firm adult control in the school often saves him from acts that might plunge him into feelings of real distress over his own behavior. But this "firm control" is not a harsh control based on arousing fear in him. It remains gentle and loving, and has within it a good deal of tolerance.

Are we saying, in effect, that David in school is different from J.W. in school because he is "allowed" to call his teacher "Dope," and J.W., because of his home training, is not? There is much truth in this, undoubtedly, yet when we look for the things that make David *want* to call his teacher and other adults "Dope," we see that he has many "reasons" for wanting to. J.W. does not have these same reasons.

In other words, even if J.W. were not disciplined by fears of punishments or by the powerful forces of coercion existing in the mores that surround him—what Flügel * calls the moral restraints—it would be difficult to picture him as a hit-run-knock-kick David. What would make him feel that way?

On the other hand, it is almost impossible to conceive of whipping or scaring David into J.W.'s state of placid compliance. For such reasons as have been pointed out, there is too much boiling emotion and need for self-assertion there below the surface seeking an outlet. As it is, his rebellious and destructive expressions must burst through some restraints. It would be wrong to picture David as a child who senses no restrictions whatever on his be-

* J. C. Flügel, *Psychoanalytic Study of the Family* (New York, International Psychoanalytical Press, 1925).

havior, just because those restrictions do not frighten or hurt him. His teacher *does* restrain him and help him learn to restrain himself. And unerringly the children in the school pick out the "difficult" child and label him "Bad Boy!" (or "Bad Girl!") though it could be sworn on a thousand Bibles that such a phrase could not possibly escape the lips of a Harriet Johnson teacher. Certainly the Harriet Johnson child's environment is not completely free from "moral" restraints, the pressure to behave in the way that society accepts.

And of course David's love for his teacher—the positive, friendly relation he has with her—in itself imposes some restraints on the urges he may have to light out and hit her when she must "interfere" with what he wants to do. The majority of instances of attacks on adults in the Harriet Johnson Nursery School, it will be remembered, were directed at the student teachers rather than at the teachers themselves. Yet David did, at times, strike even his loved teacher and order her away from him with "Go away, Dope!" His need to explode was too much for him.

We can see now that David—highly intelligent, energetic, healthy—is a child who is rather fundamentally troubled, thwarted by the circumstances of his life. In attempting to combat his situation, he does not meet with the powerful, direct restraints on his behavior that are applied to J.W. Therefore he can let himself hit and stamp and scream and destroy to some extent.

J.W. is the shy child of a shy people inhabiting a small corner of a mountain until lately almost entirely cut off from the current of life in the valleys. Less active, perhaps less intelligent, less healthy, and brought up to "behave respectfully" to his elders, J.W. cannot so easily allow himself to attack his teacher or mother as David does, but probably has such small urge to that one cannot picture him as a child whose inner life is festering with repressed rage. Adults, to J.W., may be people who whip him once in a while when he "deserves" it—and occasionally when he does not deserve it, to be sure—but certainly are not to be conceived of generally as depriving, privileged creatures who give him serious cause for rebellion, worry, and woe. On the contrary, he is king in his cabin and is allowed to gratify a great many of the strong natural urges of his early childhood.

Of course, here we are comparing him with David, the really maladjusted child. Again we say that not all children in the Harriet Johnson Nursery School are Davids. Yet most of them have some of his energy, his curiosity, his eagerness to explore, and some of his drive for brushing aside restrictions—more of this drive than the J.W.'s and Johnnie Mays have. Rebellion such as theirs does not involve maladjustment, but is the healthy expression of a desire for independence, and of a physical need to break through the physical yoke. The energy of these children, both bodily and mental, is greater than J.W.'s, the climate they live in is more conducive to activity, and ease of social contact in an exciting and often disturbing environment adds to the need for space and freedom in that space. J.W., living away off there in small Summerville, playing in his big yard at school and his familiar fields at home—unsupervised—and feeling a little tired under his hot sun, has not such a need to break down barriers. He has all the room for expansion that his less intense, less troubled kind of life requires.

And clearly, though J.W. is the gainer in one important respect, he is also a loser. He may be considered a more "secure" child than David. He has the comforting sense of belonging that is essential as a solid base to build upon. But David's gain—and Stephen's—may be in a training, completely free of fear of adults, that emphasizes growth in *self*-control; David's gain may be in a world that is wide and varied and full, a world that troubles him and excites him—and develops him; David's gain may be in a life that is characterized more by resilience and intensity, by heights and depths, than by easygoing, untroubled placidity.

ROSALIE

✿✿✿✿✿✿✿✿✿✿✿✿✿✿✿✿✿✿✿✿✿✿✿✿

IT IS NOT NECESSARY to go all the way down to the Cumberland Plateau, however, to find children who are in many ways like Johnnie May and J.W. Within easy walking distance of the Harriet Johnson Nursery School in New York City is a nursery school run by public funds—and others are scattered more distantly about the city. On these roofs, surrounded by the clangor of the streets and walled in by the adjacent masses of buildings, boys and girls are climbing and jumping and playing just as David and Stephen do. Yet they have almost as little in common with David and Stephen as our mountain children have—apparently for some of the same central reasons, in spite of the fact that the only mountains they see are skyscrapers, the only canyons city streets.

From the moment our Italian Rosalie enters her nursery school, clad in high shoes like Johnnie May's and armed with the warm kisses her mother has just poured upon her, as well as with the shrill reminder to "behave yourself and be a good girl," we can see that we have somehow wandered miles from the Harriet Johnson Nursery School in the course of only a few blocks.

Rosalie—parents on relief like Johnnie May's; Rosalie—stuffed with spaghetti as Johnnie is with biscuits; Rosalie—taken to movies as Johnnie is to buryings and revivals. Here she comes, joining her playmates who are galloping about the roof playground in the roles of G-Men or mounted police. What does a bird's eye appraisal of her reveal?

Like Johnnie, she has a brother to come to her rescue when she falls and hurts herself. He runs up to kiss the hurt place, despatching the kisses with complete confidence in their healing power.

Like Johnnie May, too, and unlike David, she settles her quarrels without screaming and without even so much as a glance
toward the teacher, appealing instead to the toughie little leader
of the group, as arbiter: "Junior hit me on the head with the
hammer."

"Well, you better hit him back."

Like Johnnie May, she seems capable of "just sitting," as she
waits placidly on a little bench for the teacher to take the group
to the playroom downstairs. Nor does she dash off and hide with
the other children when the teacher must leave them all alone for
a few moments.

Her conversation, too, as she sits crayoning with the other
four-year-olds reveals that her grammatical and verbal horizons
are more like Johnnie's than like David's or Stephen's:

"I got red! I got red!"

"I ain't got no red."

"This is gonna be nice."

"See the man?"

"I know where red are. Frow that back in."

"I'm gonna make a man."

"Look what I'm makin', now, look!"

"This is a punkin."

"Teacher, can I make another one?"

"Look what Elaine's just makin'—Elaine, that's a good one!"

"I write my name."

"How do you make that?'

"I color it and I color it."

"Look what I made, look what I made!" (singing)

"All my names!"

Her picture of a man, however, undeniably has decided originality and charm, and appears to be really quite worthy of Stephen's efforts in this direction. Are we losing sight of Johnnie
May here? Only for an instant. The teacher approaches, and once
more we are back in Summerville. For in her relationships with
her teacher Rosalie has a great deal in common with Johnnie, and

very little with those fearless Davids who resist adults without inhibition.

Watch her with her playmates over in the doll corner. Evidently these children are not playing "house." Heads bob up and down behind the screen—fingers are pointed as guns, the pitch of excitement rises, the guns r-r-r-r raucously. The teacher, hearing this rapid fire, turns and looks. Apparently the children know very well that she does not want this kind of noisy gun play down in this small room. Instantly the pointed fingers relax, the gun-fire ceases. Instantly, though the teacher has only glanced at them and taken a step or two in their direction, they comply with her wish. The doll corner no longer holds a band of machine gunners, but only a handful of small children who have no intention of defying their teacher under her very eyes and of bringing down punishment and disapproval on their heads.

This same characteristic, which might be called the tendency-to-melt-into-proper-behavior-at-the-approach-of-the-teacher, is very evident in Rosalie at rest time too, when the teacher leaves the room for a moment. Rosalie sits up, and whispers back and forth a little, and giggles softly with the others. But when teacher's footsteps are heard approaching, the sound has the effect of pushing all the children prone again, as if they were a pack of dominoes.

Clearly, eagerness to win the teacher's approval through good behavior in her presence and unwillingness to resist her, whether because of awe of adults or an easy habit of compliance that knows no need for any but the mildest rebellion, marks Rosalie off from David at every turn and identifies her as a child who has a kinship with Johnnie May.

We cannot say that Rosalie and her playmates are like Johnnie May and J.W. in every respect, however. Though there is no impression of hyperactivity in the atmosphere of their schools, still there is a good deal of activity. We do not see child after child just sitting away the morning. There are some screams. There is vigorous biffing and fighting among the children. During even a very brief visit we may hear them talking about their ages. They call each other "Dopey," though I doubt that a visitor would often hear them label a teacher with this epithet. Like the Harriet Johnson children, they can throw themselves into their play with great dramatic intensity, and at times they even burst out into rhythmic chanting. It is evident, too, that they are quite capable of producing drawings and paintings and block buildings of considerable distinction.

But the fact remains that there is a placidity, an acceptance of authority, a complete absence of biting, spitting, stamping, and wriggling away from adults that places them at once in a world far removed from David's, and not so distant from Johnnie May's.

Can we say of Rosalie what we have said of Johnnie May? That she is a child who feels the pressure of a stricter and more coercive discipline than David knows, and yet at the same time has a much smaller reservoir of resentment stored up behind the restraining dams? We cannot possibly claim for Rosalie the much less stimulating, slower-tempoed, quieter environment of a place like Summerville—nor more spacious living quarters than David's, nor a hotter sun. Possibly we can say that her health is not quite so robust as David's—she, like Johnnie May, appears to be a smaller child than David. Nor is her intelligence quotient so phenomenally high (though the majority of children scored high average or above in the Pintner-Patterson test at one of these schools).

Yet it seems self-evident that there must be other considerations. As a matter of fact, when we follow Rosalie home or watch her playing out on the sidewalks after school, we realize that in many respects her family life is similar to Johnnie May's. She lives in New York City, to be sure, just as David does, but it is a New York with which David and his parents have little or no contact.

It is not our purpose here to examine Rosalie's life in detail. Such a scrutiny would, of course, reveal many aspects of her upbringing which have little in common with either David's or Johnnie May's. For instance, though Johnnie's parents are on relief like Rosalie's, failure to pay rent in Summerville does not result in the landlord turning off the cold water, with all the attendant fuss and worry that such an inconvenience entails in Rosalie's home. It seems likely that poverty in Rosalie's family, where there are no garden plots, where flats are rented, may bring with it greater insecurity than in Johnnie's family. Furthermore, Rosalie's life includes movies, and play on the crowded, noisy city streets. Rosalie has brothers and sisters, but only one or two or three, not six or eight.

Nevertheless, it is quite possible to discern that the large pattern of Rosalie's life is cut along much the same lines as the Summerville pattern. Her family, like Johnnie May's, is a close-knit one; her place in the family is determined both by the warm affection and the authoritative type of discipline she receives.

Even a casual observer can detect the general lines of this pattern—when Rosalie's mother calls her back to plaster her with kisses before she leaves her in the morning, or admonishes her, "Don't get forward!" as she observes her behavior during the physical examination; or when the teacher remarks, "Junior's parents whipped him so hard once the neighbors called the police."

We know that in Rosalie's home the family eats together around the kitchen table. We know that mother stays home and takes care of the children and does the housework. There are no maids or nurses in the picture. We can see the children playing out on the sidewalk in the afternoons, in the care of older brothers and sisters, if mother is not free to take them to a playground. On Sunday we can watch the family going off together, perhaps to Central Park.

The whole attitude toward adults that is inculcated in the children is revealed in one remark of Rosalie's as she leaves her school on Friday afternoon: "Saturday's pay day so Monday I'll bring you a present." The small bunch of daffodils on the piano in the schoolroom, the new kerchief teacher is wearing—these are evidence that presents for Teacher really do materialize frequently, even out of extremely meager earnings.

The story of Rosalie's life is a subject for a whole book in itself. We can detect only the rough outlines of it here, yet they are sufficient to suggest that Rosalie has a somewhat greater freedom to move about in the city than is granted to David and a somewhat more intimate sharing of her parents' lives, and that undoubtedly the standards of behavior held up before her and the methods used in enforcing them are much closer to those of Summerville than of Greenwich Village.

In this connection, it is very important to observe also that Rosalie's teachers, whether consciously or not, apply the verbal pressure to "behave" in a way that is no doubt very consistent with the pressure the children receive at home, and is considerably unlike the more skillful kind of handling David receives in school: "You wet your pants, you little rascal!" "Do you think you can behave yourself if I let you stay here?" "I thought you could eat like a *big* boy." "Don't hit her, that's not nice."

To hazard the guess that Rosalie, like Johnnie, is a child whose placid school behavior is determined in large measure both by her fundamental sense of security and her awe of adults, as well as by physical considerations of health and living arrangements, probably involves very little "hazard."

It seems likely that Rosalie—who finds it so easy to "obey" her teacher, who can sit still, wait patiently in line, settle her own fights without screams—that Rosalie can stand as a check on our findings, a refutation of the common assumption that highstrung, hyperactive children like David are the products of noisy, fast-moving New York City, whereas quiet, conforming children like Johnnie May are the products of the quiet mountains.

A CONSIDERATION OF "STEPHEN"

❀❀❀❀❀❀❀❀❀❀❀❀❀❀❀❀❀❀❀❀❀

ROSALIE may corroborate our findings in another direction, if it is true that she is capable of producing paintings and drawings and block buildings of a quality somewhat superior to J.W.'s.

Throughout these pages, Stephen and David have appeared together. The Harriet Johnson children have been called both "aggressive" and "creative" in high degree, and these two characteristics have formed the major bases of comparison with the Summerville children. The reason for this has been because of the author's special interest in these aspects of behavior, not because of an implicit assumption of an inevitable relation between creative ability and the aggressiveness that is a symptom of maladjustment.

That there is some connection is probably true. It has already been suggested that the conditions giving rise to maladjustment in a proportion of the children may be the very ones that under slightly different circumstances are responsible for superior development in others. This is not to say that maladjustment itself creates or gives rise to the powers and gifts of the genius. Terman's recent studies of gifted children and his conclusions that such children are not only physically and mentally superior but come from the ranks of the emotionally stable, should lead us to question the existence of a causal relationship between instability and genius.

As a matter of fact, it is usually not David but *Stephen* at the Harriet Johnson Nursery School who is markedly gifted as painter, drawer, block builder. Thinking back to the fifteen Harriet Johnson children whom I knew well, and the room where we spent our year, I recall that the most striking paintings on our walls were generally produced by two little girls who presented no behavior problems at all to speak of. And no one could surpass Walter in drawing. Walter was the child who, as I have pointed out before, was in no way maladjusted in spite of his very high IQ.

This is not to say that the Davids had no such talents. Indeed they did. One had a marked musical gift. Another was especially expressive in rhythms. And our most architecturally beautiful block buildings were the work of a rather extraordinary little refugee child who, though not fundamentally unstable, was having considerable difficulty fitting into a world whose language he could not speak.

Yes, these children were gifted, too. Yet who can say that their accomplishments might not have been even greater if they had been more at peace with their world? My little Joanne was a child who went around with a pretty heavy chip on her shoulder. Her greatest urge seemed to be to invent little acts of retaliation. Because she was expected to be an extremely neat and orderly child at home, she was happiest when making a mess at school. The paints, to her, were something to mess with. Hurl them on the paper, mix them up, splash, dash, scrawl—and there was her picture, a good messy likeness of her troubled mood. Yet there were times when she was happier and not so driven by her vindictive spirit. On those days she was capable of approaching the easel with control and care, and her product emerged with such distinction and beauty of color and design that the adult, watching, could only gape in wonder, asking "How does she do it?" Yes, David had gifts, but Stephen's, perhaps, were more in evidence.

The question for us here revolves about Stephen and not David. What are the conditions under which he flourishes? Why is his appearance less evident among the mountain children? Here it should be emphasized that he *does* appear in a certain guise. It is not his absence that we are questioning, but the nature of this guise, which is so much less brilliant and beautiful, so much less interesting in design, than the one he wears in New York.

It is particularly easy to put one's finger on Stephen when

watching him drawing and painting, modeling, building with blocks, dancing, or when listening to him singing and talking. At the nursery school level, his originality and talent and imagination manifest themselves as he works and plays in these ways.

It would be a mistake to conceive of J.W. and Johnnie May as children who are not interested in paints, crayons, music, or who fail to attack them with spontaneity and zest and originality as Stephen does. When their shyness breaks down they, too, show themselves to be "creative" at least so far as the *process* is concerned. But we cannot speak of them as equally "creative" if we intend by that term to describe the quality of their *products.* Though J.W.'s painting may be as full of his individuality as Stephen's is of his, it does not seem to be such an interesting individuality.

The question in the long run, then, is why are J.W.'s products lacking in distinction? And to do justice to a consideration of these products, we must stop lumping them together and look at them separately. When I have spoken repeatedly of J.W.'s "inferiority," I have meant specifically that his design paintings, his drawings, his work in rhythms and in block building have not had the quality that characterized the work of the Harriet Johnson children whom I taught for a year—and of course I am using a purely subjective judgment, which may or may not be valid. Yet look at the buildings, the paintings, the drawings of the two groups side by side (and remember that all of these children have been exposed to the influence of the same teacher). The differences are not marked in the case of every child's work, yet it is not difficult to put one's finger on certain general characteristics: J.W.'s block buildings lack complexity of detail and design. They seldom have purely decorative features. "Simple enclosure" is the way I found myself most frequently describing them.

J.W.'s paintings have a hasty, technically uncontrolled look. At five and a half or six he begins to achieve the firm strokes that are Stephen's at four and a half. And even at that late age he fails to blossom forth in designs of complex geometric balance and plan, such as Anne's gleaming tree-shaped figure with its alternating branches of green and red, standing out on a solid black background. J.W.'s designs are suggested only in broad sweeps, and he seldom incorporates a whole page into a design of solid color. (Unfortunately, the paints at J.W.'s disposal were generally inferior to those provided for Stephen, in brilliance and beauty of color. Sometimes, indeed, J.W. had nothing more to work with than the juice of poke berries and a reddish-brown liquid made from the native clay. It may not be too much to say that some of the magnificent effects achieved by the Harriet Johnson Stephens were the purely accidental result of the juxtaposition of magnificent colors.)

J.W.'s drawings are more frequently in the scribble stage than the four-year-old Stephen's. He never emerges with a drawing of a house, an animal, or a man that includes such detail as Stephen's. Four-and-a-half-year-old Buddy's picture of "Miss Lewis" consists of an enormous head with three octopuslike legs a-dangling. But four-and-a-half-year-old Deborah's portrait entitled "Miss Lewis in Her Flowered Smock" not only includes the flowers but heels on the shoes, the brown skirt hanging below the smock, pink cheeks and lips. (I do not mean to imply that the octopus version is without its charm!) Furthermore, J.W. seldom fills a page with solid color. "Sketchy lines" are characteristic of him.

And J.W. in rhythms, as has been pointed out before, is to Stephen as a tortoise to a gazelle; as a man on a crutch to a creature with wings. But J.W. singing and talking—another matter. I should certainly hesitate to claim that J.W.'s ability to carry a tune or that his delight in singing a song is any less than Stephen's. In fact, though "chanting" was conspicuously absent, spontaneous singing of learned songs was more in evidence in the mountain school than in the city school, and nowhere could there have been more delighted listening to songs—if they were the "right" kind sung in the "right" way!

Five-year-old Earldine pulls her chair up to the stove and rocks her doll to sleep. She begins to sing the ballad she calls "The Polished Steps." This is no childish piping. This is ballad-singing in a loud, clear, mountain voice. The other children hear her and are drawn to her. They bring up their chairs and sit around her, listening. She sings them one ballad after another, for fifteen or twenty minutes, before they tire of sitting. This is real entertainment for them. (I reflected as I listened to them—not without the bitterness of one who must bow to a rival!—that the children had never shown such interest in listening to the little children's songs about trains, wagons, horsies, and so on, that I was in the habit of singing to them. I think Earldine's rendition of "The Polished Steps" marked the beginning of my policy of abandoning most of the typical nursery school songs in favor of folk songs and ballads—though I never did achieve the nasal twang and was more than once abashed by a child's frank comment, "You don't know how to sing!")

Not only did the mountain children sing the ballads and hymns they knew, but sometimes they made up original variations. One day Edna came to school booming out, to the tune of the Crawdad Song: "Old Man Clay ate a bale of hay, Baby!" Not a masterpiece, to be sure, but her own song about her next door neighbor. And it was Edna who made up what I called the Howdy Song, for singing as we were riding to or from school in the car. It was nothing but a greeting to the people—and things—we passed, sung in a rambling way to familiar tunes:

> Howdy, old woman!
> Howdy, old horse,
> Howdy, Geneva's house,
> Howdy, Susie's house!

Yes, J.W. is a music lover, certainly no less than Stephen. I should hesitate to state categorically that his joy in the sounds and rhythms of words and the patterns of stories is less than Stephen's, too, or that his ability to use words and sounds with imaginative insight is inherently a mediocre one. Such ability, I think, was somewhat undeveloped in the beginning, but as I have pointed out, flowered surprisingly under encouragement in the course of two years. Wayne Edward's ears were as keen as Stephen's when he told me that the squeak of the tricycle was like the rooster crowin' in the mornin'. Buddy was just as skilled in his ability to manipulate sound when he "heard" the windshield wiper saying "chip-chop, chip-chop," when he told me that the water spilling over on the hot stove was saying "h-u-sh!"

The Summerville children invented a number of little games or chants which revolved around the sounds of words and amounted to nothing but delight in those sounds. There was a period when an onlooker would have seen the children clutching little bunches of oak leaves as they climbed into the car each day. The game was to hold these leaves out of the window of the car just far enough to let the wind click and rustle them together. The sound—and possibly the appearance, too—suggested fighting chickens to the children, and the "game" would not have been complete without the little chant to accompany it:

> *My* chickens are *fight*in',
> *My* chickens are *fight*in'.

Another game of more or less spontaneous origin became a kind of ritual just before lunch each day. The children lay on their cots watching me finish the lunch preparations. When I began to pour out the soup, it was their signal. "Is it ready? Is it ready? Is it ready?" they asked, over and over in low, slow, controlled voices, not in unison by any means, but in counterpoint. It was not really a question they were asking. It was not *talk* but a *sound*, startlingly like the gentle clacking of leaves in a wind.

Singing, and the spoken word. It is significant that artistically the Summerville children reached their greatest heights in these two media. Significant, and yet not at all surprising. For after all, these are the media most familiar to them, those that are a part of their tradition, their everyday living. Singing is more alive, probably, in a Summerville home than a Greenwich Village home. The ballads and hymns brought to school by the children are not plucked out of thin air, but are learned at home from parents who sing as they go about their work. And Wayne Edward's pleasure in the sound of "Chickens Squawk, That's what!" and his ability (finally!) to conceive of quietness as "quiet as you go after a chicken" are not unrelated to his knowledge of a common spoken language that is rich in expressiveness, that often achieves an almost poetic quality of clear vision.

Listen to the Summerville people in casual conversation. These are the bits you overhear:

". . . and when the lightnin' struck it dug a ditch deep enough to bury this baby in!" "We dyed a whole rafter of burlap and it was plum pretty." "He'd have no more chance in New York than a hog on the main line." ". . . and then when spring opens up . . ." "When you try to hold the baby she'll scrammish around on your lap." "She walks so fast, her little legs just a-reachin' out!" "Hit's a spit snow." "This mornin' I put a gap in my foot *that* deep!" "Her little feet was cold as frogs."

Old Aunt Mag meets Mr. Smith in town and greets him:

> "Howdy, Ernest, how are you?"
> "On top of the world, and you?"
> "Oh, I'm able to get to the table."

Mr. Henderson calls in the cows in a rather mournful, musical drawl: "Sook, heifer, sook—sook—sook—"

Whereas the chickens come to his wife's more sprightly: "*Chickee, chickee, chickee-ee-ee-ee-e?*"

The Summerville children even have some acquaintance with little verses and rhymes—of a kind! It was an odd assortment that I collected from them, ranging from Horace's catalog, which he used to reel off at unpredictable times during the day:

> Apples, peaches, peanut butter!

to Ina Lee's "poem" from an old song:

> Little boy, little boy,
> Where'd you get your breeches?
> Ma cut 'em out
> And Pa sewed the stitches.

Ina Lee had a rhythmic little "catalog," too, to match against Horace's:

> Silk, satin, calico, cotton!

—as well as a little piece of a refrain:

> Cowbells, cowbells,
> Ringin' in my ears.

And for days Wayne Edward delighted in quoting a rhyme that he said he learned from his sister:

> Dickle Dackle Doo!
> I got a pony will run YOU!

No great verses, these, but evidence that pleasure in sounds and rhythms of words is not as unknown in the Summerville cabins as might be supposed.

Now rhythms, block building, painting, drawing—these are another story. I think that very few of the nursery school children had held crayons or paint brushes in their hands before they had the opportunity to do so at the school. I doubt that Summerville ever produced an artist, in the sense of one who paints and draws. Every housewife makes quilts that are attractive as well as useful; everybody sings; Uncle Mac makes furniture that is pleasing to look at; Alexander writes verses for radio broadcasting; a number of people play "git-tars" and fiddles; Jim Priest whittles little figures out of cedar wood and has even started to write a book; Summerville housewives do not hesitate to act in the plays put on by the P.T.A.—plays chosen from a list in a catalog.

There are arts in Summerville, but they seem not to include painting and drawing.

Who could afford to buy paints and brushes and canvases? Who, of these miners and lumbermen? It costs nothing to sing. It costs nothing to put together a quilt out of the scraps that are at hand, or to whittle a piece of wood. And who could afford to buy pictures to decorate the cabins, pictures or beautiful rugs and books and china? The interior of the average Summerville cabin is as completely devoid of objects of color, form, and beauty as is a barn, except for the quilts on the beds, and sometimes even the quilts have lost much of their original brightness. Exteriors, too, it must be remembered, seldom bear any resemblance to the idealized picture one may have in mind of the beautifully constructed log cabin nestling among great overhanging trees at the side of the mountain.

Summerville children have neither a tradition of painting and drawing to give them encouragement, nor any acquaintance with artistic surroundings—a fact that may not be entirely unrelated to their ability or inability to paint and draw. Outside of quilting, none of the mountain handicrafts that are often considered a part of Southern mountain culture has developed to any extent in Summerville, not sufficiently, that is, to become a part of a living, flourishing tradition. Even the art of quilting lags far behind the heights reached in some mountain communities. It seems likely that where the mountain handicrafts have developed extensively, there has always been encouragement in the form of a settlement or school in the neighborhood devoted to rejuvenation not only of the arts but of the whole life of the community.

The Highlander Folk School has not always been able to function in this capacity, strictly as a community school, since its purpose is to serve as an educational center for working people from all parts of the South. Nor has its primary function ever been exclusively that of bringing about a cultural renaissance of the folk arts. Primarily it has attempted to help the mountain people, and all those who have come to its doors from all over the South, to attack their desperate economic problem at the roots. It has felt that encouragement of a strong labor movement would ultimately bring more rejuvenation in its wake than encouragement of arts and crafts alone.

When it has had the time and the facilities, it has indeed served as a cultural as well as an educational and social center for the community of Summerville. The square dancing of the neighborhood owes its revival to the influence of the Folk School, and at various times other activities have undoubtedly received considerable impetus from the presence of the Folk School in Summerville. It is not unlikely that quilting, for instance, is entering into a new and flowering phase of development at the present time, as the result of the activity of the small Cooperative organized with the help of the Folk School. The members are ferreting out the best old designs of the locality, and are making quilts for sale.

For the majority of Summerville families, however, it is still true to say that, with the exception of singing, cultural activities have little place in their lives, and for the majority of homes it is largely true to say that there is nothing, nothing of beauty in them.

It may not be too much to hope, however, that the devoted efforts of the schoolteacher, Miss Justus, may bear some fruit when the young people who were under her influence for many years set up their own homes, as a few are now beginning to do. It cannot be said of these children that they have not learned to plait rugs and baskets, to make household ornaments of metal and wood; it cannot be said of them that they have never known pride in tending a flower garden. And undoubtedly they have been introduced to a world of story, song, and poetry which seldom is brought to rural children in isolated regions.

At the present time it remains true, however, that the set of visual stimuli characterizing J.W.'s surroundings is vastly inferior to that to which Stephen and David are exposed. Paintings hang on the walls of the Greenwich Village homes, and in these homes the arrangement, design, and color of furnishings have all been planned with an eye for beauty. Every Stephen's room has its shelf of beautifully illustrated books.

And is there any significance in the fact that Stephen, at times, looks up to the Chrysler tower and the Empire State (as well as to the hideous conglomeration of the grimy-bricked backs of apartments)? He sees, at times, the graceful curve of the George

Washington Bridge; (also the cluttered, narrow streets of Greenwich Village). He has walked beneath the arch in Washington Square (and past rows of ash cans and garbage cans on the sidewalks). He can see the spires and towers of churches, the huge, receding, angular masses of the skyscrapers of New York. What a myriad of shapes and forms—both ugly and beautiful—unknown to J.W.! Of course, J.W. sees more sky, and knows well the colors and movements of leaves, grasses, clouds, animals. Yet these are not entirely unknown to Stephen, as skyscrapers are unknown to J.W. In fact, Stephen may see more horses on the streets of New York than J.W. sees in Summerville!

Furthermore, David and Stephen, from their early childhood, have been encouraged to paint and draw. Their parents not only have a lively interest in art but may be artists themselves. Crayons, paper, easels, paints are a standard part of the Harriet Johnson child's home "play" equipment. He has had the practice and encouragement that no one has been able to give to J.W. This element of "practice" with a technique is of considerable importance, and is not such a matter for speculation as is the question of the effect of surroundings on the perceptive eye of the child.

Stephen's jewel-like designs were not produced on the first day of school—nor even in the first month or two or three. They were the culmination of seven or eight months, or more, of daily experimentation. (Most of the four-year-olds in my group had been in the school one or two years before they came to me.)

Mary's delightful, original crayon-box faces were not a spontaneous invention, but were the gradual outgrowth of nothing more than a line drawn around the little oblong crayon box as it rested on her paper. For days she was content to trace and cut out these oblongs. Then one day she happened to place a few dots inside, suggesting a face. Later she added sprigs of "hair" curling out on all sides, till after a while emerged the one and only crayon-box face.

Harriet Johnson children progressed through smears and scribbles and wobbly lines to firmness and control and intricate plan. Summerville children progressed too, but they were necessarily several laps behind. The children who were four and five when they entered the school had to begin at the beginning—where Stephen started when he was two or three.

Those who had two years of solid "practice" in painting—and there weren't many, since paints were not available in the Summerville nursery school during the first six months—in the end were much closer to Stephen's achievement than the children who had had less opportunity to find their way through indeterminate strokes to something more controlled.

As it was, many of J.W.'s later pictures were considered interesting and very beautiful by Highlander staff members who had no knowledge of the Harriet Johnson pictures as a basis of comparison. Perhaps it is too soon to say that J.W. could never equal Stephen in painting and drawing. Given the tools, the time to practice—in short, the long *encouragement*—he might.

Why does Stephen excel in block building? Does his familiarity with the architecture of New York have something to do with his wonderful ability to place block on block in a structure of intricate grace and balance?

Primarily, I think this ability of his is related to another factor. Stephen—say, a four-year-old Stephen—when he rushes to the shelves for an armful of blocks, eager to get to work, is probably not saying to himself (nor even remotely thinking!) "Now I'm going to make a beautiful building." He does not usually build in the abstract like that, but in the first place is motivated to get the blocks because he wants to make something he has seen. He has been to the dock with the other children. He wants to make that huge liner! He has been to the stables. He wants to make a stable so that he can have fun playing with the toy horses, walking them up his play ramp just like the real horses walked up the real, big ramp. Blocks, to Stephen, are primarily materials with which to reconstruct the things he sees around him in which he is interested. Often, to be sure, he elaborates on his original idea and ends up with a decorative structure of no function except to delight in.

As I have suggested previously, it seems quite likely that the environment of New York City offers a good deal more for block builders than the rural environment of Summerville. That is not to say that in itself it need be a richer sort of environment, but merely that it is one which lends itself extremely well to architectural reproduction.

What is there for J.W. to build? Cabins, barns, roads, trains, a garage, a store, a schoolhouse, a church, a Folk School. What else? Of course he is interested in a thousand more things—in rabbits and squirrels, in the hog-killin', in the tadpoles in the brook, in hunting for holly in the woods—but you can't build these things out of blocks.

Stephen, on the other hand, has a never-ending supply of buildings to choose from: stores of great variety, apartments, fire stations, boats, docks, bridges, skyscrapers, stables, hospitals, markets, steamshovels, snoweaters, trains and tracks, churches, theaters, barber shops, shoe shining stands, pet shops, elevated railways, subways, parks, aquaria, and so on and on. With a greater stimulus to build in the first place, Stephen develops greater skill than J.W., who does not have such an urge to handle the blocks.

Of course, as all teachers know, there is something of a "chance" element in a good block building program, too, depending on whether or not a large proportion of children in the group "take to" the blocks more readily than to some of the other materials. One or two or three children who are especially interested in block building play can draw the others in. "Who wants to have a hospital so this ambulance can take these people to it? Who will build a station because my train has to unload all this freight?"

There were times at the Summerville Nursery School when there were many block buildings on the floor each day, a result of the enthusiasm of certain children who were new in the group, and eager to try their hand with the blocks. These times were not always of very long duration, however, because of the fluctuating nature of the children's attendance at the school.

Artistry in block building is like that in painting and drawing. It develops as a result of practice. Children can only achieve

complex forms in blocks when they have learned how to master
the fundamental techniques of bridging, enclosing, and generally
getting the feel of the blocks. It was not really incongruous at
all that five-year-old J.W., when he first tried his hand with the
blocks, could make nothing more elaborate than one of three-
year-old Stephen's attempts. It must be remembered that Stephen
has a set of blocks at home, too, just like the standard nursery
school blocks. His experience in block building has been a much
longer one than J.W.'s both at home and at school.

I have been told that the nursery school children in the rural
community of Arthurdale * in West Virginia were wonderful
block builders. It is logical that they should have been. This is
the community where stranded miners were being resettled in
new homesteads. The construction of new homes, new schools,
new buildings (of an architectural type completely different
from anything in their past experience) was going on near the
school daily. A new life was in the making, and the children were
there in the midst of it. No wonder that they took to their blocks
eagerly, as a way of digesting all the exciting new sights that had
suddenly come into their ken. And no wonder that they developed skill and artistry as a result.

There was no such hum of excitement and activity in Summerville. If I had been able to take the children to the outlying
towns more frequently, to seek for what was not in our own community, the history of block building in the Summerville school
might have taken a somewhat different course.

When we consider J.W.'s performance in rhythms, we must
again think of the traditions of Summerville. Rhythmic dancing that is full body expression has no part in these traditions.
But as for Stephen—his mother may be one of the leading "modern dancers" of our time.

Even square dancing does not flourish in Summerville without
encouragement. And as it is done by the mountain people, it is
decidedly a restrained art of movement. It demands no bursting
forth from the shell of shy reserve. It is dancing with the feet

* Elsie R. Clapp, *Community Schools in Action* (New York, Viking Press, 1939).

and knees, not with the whole body. One can even retain one's habitual facial expression and get through the dance very well. It is not necessary to smile, to show animation, vigor, and good spirits. When I think of "square dance at Highlander Folk School," the picture that flashes into my mind is of a crowded room, benches around the walls filled with solemn-faced women and girls and sleeping babies and children; boys and men standing in a bunch over by the door, and dancing sets whirling smoothly around in the middle of the room to the mountain "git-tar" music that defies description. Laughter and kicking and calling are provided by the "outsiders" who are taking part, the students or visitors who are not mountain people. Their dancing is vastly inferior, to be sure. Not one of them achieves the smooth, masterly, controlled glide of the mountain boys. Perhaps that is a significant difference. The outsiders try to enter in as though it were really vigorous "dancing." To the mountain people it is a matter of gliding, smooth-stepping, achieved with a minimum of extraneous motion.

The rhythmic dancing of the nursery school aims at something quite different—something that a shy, reserved, self-conscious person cannot well take part in. It is not difficult to see why J.W. does not take to it as easily as Stephen does. He is shy, he is not endowed with an abundance of physical vigor, and there has been nothing in his tradition to encourage such activity. Even the fact that he has no everyday familiarity with the piano music used for accompaniment may partially explain his hesitance.

Yet J.W. has a sense of rhythm. He has a sense of design and delight in color. He is capable, at times, of constructing beautiful block buildings. What is lacking?

To some extent it may be fair to say that Summerville children are just not endowed with the particular gifts that are Stephen's. To some extent we can, perhaps, trace the differences to a physical basis. We know that in his general physical development J.W. lags far behind Stephen. We know that his store of energy is far less. This has a great deal to do with his responses in rhythms, and suggests also that J.W. may fall behind not only in the muscular control but in the visual functions allied to success in painting and drawing.

To some extent we can say that the pressures and taboos which aim to make J.W. control his aggressive expressions, to make him "behave" in the presence of his teacher, may help to create the initial shy restraint in him which for a time extends into all of his muscles and inhibits every part of his behavior, not only his aggressive urges.

To some extent, in the cases of a few children, we can say that an unduly harsh discipline or exposure to frightening threats and roughness may have bottled up spontaneity, may have made for an atmosphere unfavorable to the development and free expression of originality.

Yet of far more importance than any one factor in explaining the quality of the majority of the children's accomplishments, lacking as they are not in spontaneity but in distinction, is the total picture of their life in Summerville. Their environment, failing to provide the stimulating, complex, invigorating, many-faceted kind of living that develops depth and breadth and intensity in the personalities of those who inhabit Stephen's home, has not been favorable to the growth of certain abilities. It has offered neither the traditions and encouragement nor the opportunity for "practice" that Stephen has had. I am not sure that J.W., if he lived in Stephen's Greenwich Village, might not achieve more of Stephen's results. As it is, where he has received a constant encouragement, where his efforts are in line with a living tradition, he has accomplished wonders.

If it is true that Rosalie's skill in drawing, painting, block building is somewhat greater than J.W.'s (and I have not a sufficiently close acquaintance with her work to state categorically that it is), it may be for this very reason: she lives in a New York which, though not quite the same as Greenwich Village, offers her encouragement.

At this point one stops and asks, have the arts of painting, sculpture, poetry, architecture, music, ever come to high fruition in isolated rural communities where the participants were cut off from and unable to steep themselves in the traditions of those arts?

And what keeps these traditions alive in the places where they do flourish? Could it be that the arts thrive on the friction that results when ideas meet and clash, when mind and emotion are vigorously stimulated at every turn? Is there a relation between the placid porch-sitting of Summerville, the even monotony of the day-by-day existence, and the absence of superior achievement in the arts? Is there a relation between the Village energy and activity, the Village urge for highest development of the individual, and the fact that many Village parents are artists of the first order?

This is not to say that, nor even to ask whether, maladjustment is essential to artistic production. It is not a question of maladjustment but of conflict, of stimulus, of social give and take, of ambition and desire, that may or may not lead to a poor adjustment on the part of the individuals involved. Nor is this to imply that "life" can only be lived in the large cities, and that there can be no conflict, no arts of any kind, and no experience of active participation in them in the country regions.

Summerville people know death and love and sickness and birth. In Summerville there is a struggle for food, a struggle for jobs; and the bitter realization comes to many a family that the jobs dangle, sometimes, on threads held by politicians; the bitter realization, too, that there may be discrimination against the man who joins the union. The ingredients of "life" exist in Summerville as in New York. Perhaps what is lacking is a match to put the flame there. With consistent leadership, closer community organization, a common purpose, and especially with a broader knowledge and a desire and *hope* for something better, Summerville might stir itself—and incidentally might boast of ballad makers of the first order, of fiddlers and carvers and quilters in the best tradition of the folk arts.

As a matter of fact, there have been times when Summerville community spirit has run high; when the people have been brought together and fired by a common disaster. This was the case during the period when so many of the men were cut off W.P.A. as the result of a politician's quarrel; during that long demonstration when men, women, and children camped in the W.P.A. office in Dyersville, cooking, eating, sleeping there, demanding soberly and firmly their jobs. There was a stirring play, too, at that time, on an outdoor stage at the Folk School, not a play with memorized lines, but the spontaneous story of the W.P.A. demonstration, and the actors were the Summerville men and women who had been through it all.

The nursery school also brought the community together to a certain extent, in providing a number of families, at times, with something of a focal point, something to fight for and stand together for. Moreover there are families who are considerably more active in the community than others; families who have maintained a fairly close relation with the Folk School. Among them there is less porch-sitting.

It is very true that Summerville is a far cry from the community it undoubtedly would be if there had never been a Folk School in its midst, nor a Dr. Lillian Johnson, nor a May Justus. Summerville is not a Colvin Hollow,* where complete isolation and complete complacency have resulted in complete lethargy. Yet neither is it an Arthurdale, where hope for life on a new and more solid economic basis changed the course of events for every family, and quickened the pulse of the community.

The existence of conflict, of art, of "life," seems to be not so much a matter of city versus country as it is of social and intellectual contact versus isolation; awareness and purpose versus ignorance and a dulled indifference. Perhaps, also, comparative financial abundance versus an abundance of poverty just above the desperation line is at the very base of the total picture.

It becomes increasingly clear that "adjustment" or "emotional stability" in Greenwich Village is apt to involve something more than "stability" in Summerville. It becomes clear that there may be various levels of adjustment. The Harriet Johnson child who is secure and untroubled may be a rather different child from the

* See Sherman and Henry, *Hollow Folk* (New York, Thomas Y. Crowell Co., 1933).

untroubled J.W., both at six and at sixteen. "Stability" in Summerville may involve little pain. It can be the stability of the pond that is not greatly disturbed. "Stability" achieved in Greenwich Village at the crossroads, so to speak, with the breakers beating at the receding shore, is another matter. It can be considered adjustment on a higher level, if one values high artistic accomplishment and high intelligence, with the sensitivity that it implies.

CONCLUSIONS

✿✿✿✿✿✿✿✿✿✿✿✿✿✿✿✿✿✿✿✿✿✿✿✿✿✿

I WANTED TO MAKE this study of J.W. versus David and Stephen to satisfy my curiosity as to why the mountain children were so different from the Greenwich Village children. But also, in the back of my mind there was the question whether J.W.'s apparently much less troubled life meant that it was a better kind of life.

It has become clear to me that it is not possible to say, "The placidity of the Summerville children is entirely a good thing." A more or less negative type of security turns out to be a rather high price to pay for the avoidance of turmoil. Clearly conflict itself is not the thing to be feared but, rather, the denial or absence of it, the inability to deal with it. Sacrifice David and you must sacrifice Stephen too.

Does the unfrustrated placidity, the small peaceful life of the Summerville children give them a poise that stays with them as they grow up? Does it equip them with the power and strength and resilience to deal with disappointment, to adjust to new experiences? I think of Helen who returns from Chicago, homesick; of the boys and girls who drop out of the high school, unable to cope with the difficulties it presents; of the adults who bicker, quarrel and flare up like wild cats at the scratch of a pin.

Does the Summerville soil nurture the artist? It is in the atmosphere provided by his stimulating, albeit disturbing, parents that Stephen flourishes. And it is through his troubles and by means of his aggressiveness that David may work his way out to a high level of adjustment. For who is the better adjusted, Julia who goes so unrebelliously through the school day, yet is frozen with hesitation when she is taken over to the strange Highlander Folk School, or Cullen who, though he cannot sit still and may dash off down the hall away from his teacher, has no fear of approaching the workmen in the street to ask why they are boring a hole there?

Who is the better adjusted, Julia who is in a panic when she must see the doctor, or Carl who goes through a two weeks' siege with an eye operation and emerges calmly; who, though he comes to school wearing most strange dark glasses with a little slit cut to look through (the children call them "pirate glasses") can explain to his classmates philosophically that the reason he is wearing them is to help his eyes when he grows up, so he can drive automobiles and read books?

Who is up against a situation demanding an adjustment, J.W. or my four-year-old David—and for once I am speaking of the real David, the real child I knew who is back of this symbolic name—David who was finding it extremely difficult not to have his way in every little matter? He was a pathetically unhappy, fearful little fellow. Perhaps his insistence that his every thought and act must stand unchallenged was one of his ways of trying to gather up a little strength unto himself. It led him into absurd and almost unbelievable situations. One day, I remember, I was reading a story to the children about some Scottie dogs. We came to the part where the father dog had to stay out of the room where the baby dogs were because fathers were too jumpy and noisy and didn't understand how to act around babies. David flared right up, defending his father, asserting that his father was *not* noisy and jumpy.

Miss Lewis: "But David, this means the father *dog!*"

David, determinedly: "Well, my father *is* a father dog!"

If David learns to give in to others eventually, to recognize error in himself, he will indeed have achieved "adjustment," perhaps a good deal more so than J.W. who has never felt the props slipping from under him, as David has.

He may achieve the kind of adjustment that Joseph has already effected, Joseph who, when he came to the Harriet Johnson Nursery School at the age of four, had already lived in Berlin, Istanbul, and New York, and could speak both French and German. The boy was like a fire engine out of control for the first few months of his astounding career in our room. Unable to speak English, he jabbered nonsense at the top of his voice; frustrated and beside himself that he could not entirely master his new environment, he would fling himself down on the floor and spin around, shuffle and roar and race about. Yet at the end of six months Joseph was speaking English fairly well, was calming down, and had made himself an accepted and popular leader of the group. He had been determined to learn the things the others knew. When they built a shoe-shine stand and had no room for him to play with them, he observed them carefully and built a shoe-shine stand of his own just like theirs, if not a little better. In short, Joseph emerged from that temporary maelstrom with a great strong stride, a robust nature. Is this "adjustment" that he finally achieved any different from the "adjustment" of a J.W. who has never been up against the necessity to make a place for himself in a completely alien world?

To be sure, Joseph had a solid prop beneath him, without which he might not have been able to build that rather amazing edifice. He had what J.W. has—confidence in his parents, warmth, love, a sense of belonging in the safe world of his home, wherever that home might be.

No, now that this study is made I am not packing my trunks with the intent of moving down to Tennessee, building me a cabin, taking to the "simple life" and rearing my hypothetical children in the way the Summerville families do. For us it is not a question of attempting to turn the clock back in that way, which, indeed, would be as impossible as it would be undesirable. It is rather a question of trying to bring to Greenwich Village a little more of the one superior ingredient in Summerville life, for the lack of which David so frequently flounders.

There is no one way to do it. I have no easy, infallible set of rules to present. There is no one way to impart warmth, to implant confidence and trust, to insure love. Certainly it is not through any mechanical means easily listed as 1, 2, 3, but through their genuine interest in their children, through their respect and love for them, however it may be expressed, that Village parents succeed in avoiding the possible pitfalls for children in their way of life.

Yet undoubtedly a close attention to some of the more mechanical details does help achieve the successes—a careful selection of nursemaids, for instance, a premium on as much space as possible in living quarters, an arrangement of the schedule that will allow for as much time as possible for the family to be together, to eat together, go out together.

And undoubtedly at least one specific point can be made about all children who are happy, unafraid, at peace with their world, whether they live in Summerville or Greenwich Village or anywhere else. Surely it can be said that their parents have all at some time or other made it a practice to take them along to "help drive home the cow," even after dark.

BIBLIOGRAPHY

❀❀❀❀❀❀❀❀❀❀❀❀❀❀❀❀❀❀❀❀❀❀❀

American Public Welfare Association. Public Welfare and Related Problems in Grundy Co., Tennessee. Chicago, 1940.

Bentley, J. E. Superior Children. New York, W. W. Norton and Co., 1937.

Biber, Barbara. Children's Drawings: from Lines to Pictures. Bureau of Educational Experiments, The Cooperating School Pamphlets, No. 6. New York, 1934.

Campbell, John Charles. The Southern Highlander and His Homeland. New York, Russell Sage Foundation, 1921.

Clapp, Elsie Ripley. Community Schools in Action. New York, Viking Press, 1939.

Davis, Allison, and John Dollard. Children of Bondage. Washington, D.C., American Council on Education, 1940.

Dennis, Wayne. The Hopi Child. New York, Appleton-Century, 1940.

Dewey, John. Art as Experience. New York, Minton Balch and Co., 1934.

Dollard, John. Criteria for the Life History. New Haven, Yale University Press, 1936.

—— and Others. Frustration and Aggression. New Haven, Yale University Press, 1939.

Edwards, A. S., and L. Jones. "An Experimental and Field Study of North Georgia Mountaineers." *J. Soc. Psychol.*, IX (1938), 317–333.

Enslow, Ella. Schoolhouse in the Foothills. New York, Simon and Schuster, 1935.

Flügel, J. C. Psychoanalytic Study of the Family. International Psychoanalytical Library, Stechert and Co., New York, 1925.

Griffiths, Ruth. Imagination in Early Childhood. London, Kegan Paul, Trench, Trubner and Co. Ltd., 1938.

Horney, Karen. The Neurotic Personality of Our Time. New York, W. W. Norton and Co., 1937.

—— New Ways in Psychoanalysis. New York, W. W. Norton and Co., 1939.

Horowitz, E. L., and R. E. Horowitz. "Development of Social Attitudes in Children." *Sociometry*, I (1937–38), 301–337.

Johnson, Harriet M. The Art of Block Building. New York, John Day Co., 1933.

Kardiner, Abram. The Individual and His Society. New York, Columbia University Press, 1939.

Levy, John, and Ruth Munroe. The Happy Family. New York, Alfred A. Knopf, 1938.

Lynd, Robert S., and Helen M. Lynd. Middletown. New York, Harcourt, Brace and Co., 1929.

—— Middletown in Transition. New York, Harcourt, Brace and Co., 1937.

Mead, Margaret. Coming of Age in Samoa. New York, William Morrow and Co., 1928.

—— Growing Up in New Guinea. New York, William Morrow and Co., 1930.

—— Sex and Temperament. New York, William Morrow and Co., 1935.

Murphy, G., L. B. Murphy, and T. M. Newcomb. Experimental Social Psychology. (Revised edition.) New York, Harper and Bros., 1937.

Plant, James S. Personality and the Cultural Pattern. New York, The Commonwealth Fund, 1937.

Sheppard, Muriel E. Cabins in the Laurel. Chapel Hill, N.C., University of North Carolina Press, 1935.

Sherman, Mandel, and C. B. Key. "The Intelligence of Isolated Mountain Children. *Child Development,* III (1932), 279–290.

Sherman, Mandel, and Thomas R. Henry. Hollow Folk. New York, Thomas Y. Crowell Co., 1933.

Stern, Bernhard J. The Family, Past and Present. New York, Appleton-Century, 1938.

Terman, Lewis M. Genetic Studies of Genius. 2 vols. Palo Alto, Calif., Stanford University Press, 1925. Vol. I.

Travis, Lee L. Speech Pathology. New York, D. Appleton and Co., 1931.

Ware, Caroline F. Greenwich Village, 1920–1930. Boston, Houghton Mifflin Co., 1935.

INDEX

❀❀❀❀❀❀❀❀❀❀❀❀❀❀❀❀❀❀❀❀❀❀❀